T0044957

# After the Crisis

*For Simonetta, because this book
has stolen some of our time together*

# After the Crisis

*Alain Touraine*

Translated by Helen Morrison

Polity

First published in French as *Après la crise* © Editions du Seuil, 2010

This English edition © Polity Press, 2014

Polity Press
65 Bridge Street
Cambridge CB2 1UR, UK

Polity Press
350 Main Street
Malden, MA 02148, USA

ISBN-13: 978-0-7456-5384-6
ISBN-13: 978-0-7456-5385-3 (pb)

A catalogue record for this book is available from the British Library.

Typeset in 11 on 13 pt Berling by
Servis Filmsetting Ltd, Stockport, Cheshire
Printed and bound in Great Britain by T.J. International, Padstow, Cornwall

The publisher has used its best endeavours to ensure that the URLs for external websites referred to in this book are correct and active at the time of going to press. However, the publisher has no responsibility for the websites and can make no guarantee that a site will remain live or that the content is or will remain appropriate.

Every effort has been made to trace all copyright holders, but if any have been inadvertently overlooked the publisher will be pleased to include any necessary credits in any subsequent reprint or edition.

For further information on Polity, visit our website: www.politybooks.com

# Contents

# Acknowledgements

This book, which has appeared in a number of successive versions, meant an enormous amount of work which was superbly undertaken by my research assistants Christelle Ceci, Émilie Ronflard and Aurélien Bergerat. May they be the first to be thanked. Yvon Le Bot kindly agreed to proof-read the text and corrected many errors.

I had promised Olivier Bétourné, who had encouraged my work over the course of many years, that this text would follow him to whichever publishing house his personal history took him. I am delighted that his return to the Éditions du Seuil in the role of president has given me the chance to work once again with the editor of the first half of my professional life.

In CADIS, which I founded in 1981, and particularly in the person of Michel Wieviorka, who took over from me as director from 1993 to 2009, I have always found an intellectual support which I have valued enormously. May the work we carried out over a period of twenty-eight years be continued under Philippe Bataille, the new director of CADIS.

I am particularly grateful to friends from other countries who have chosen to establish close links in terms both of work and of friendship with CADIS and with myself: Manuel Castells (Spain), Manuel Antonio Garretón (Chile), Bernard Francq and Geoffrey Pleyers (Belgium), Danièle Joly (Great Britain), Kevin McDonald (Australia and Great Britain), Julio Labastida Del Campo, Maria Eugenia Sánchez, Ilan Bizberg and Sergio Zermeño (Mexico), Denis Sulmont (Peru),

Fernando Calderón (Argentina and Bolivia), Antimo Farro and Alberto Meluccit (Italy), Mi Ran and Soo Bok Sheong (South Korea), Laura Faxas (Dominican Republic), Louis Maheu (Quebec), Tom Dwyer (New Zealand and Brazil), President Fernando Henrique and Rutht Cardoso and José Arthur Gianotti (Brazil), Torcuato di Tella, Liliana De Ris and José Nun (Argentina), Francisco Zapata and Maria Luisa Tarres (Chile and Mexico). Finally, I can never sufficiently thank Jacqueline Blayac and Jacqueline Longerinas with whom I have worked for so long.

# Introduction

'That there will be changes as a result of the crisis is certain. There is no going back to the world before the crisis. But the questions are, how deep and fundamental will the changes be? Will they even be in the right direction? We have lost the sense of urgency, and what has happened so far does not portend well for the future.'

Joseph Stiglitz, *Freefall*, 2010, p. 295

An economic crisis is first and foremost a matter for economists. Even if they have not always succeeded in predicting them in advance, economists have analysed crises in detail, examining their causes, how they unfold, their consequences and the attempts made to recover from them or to avoid the worst of their impact. Economists were responsible for numerous books on the 2007–9 financial crisis and its causes, some aimed at professionals and others at a wider public. A certain number of them struck a chord in popular opinion.

It would, however, be absurd to claim that sociologists should confine themselves simply to studying the non-economic factors of the economic situation. Such a concern has always been part of economic thinking, whether in the context of the early twentieth-century 'institutionalist' school and the current school of regulation or in the work of Joseph Schumpeter – and even as far back as Adam Smith. Moreover, a large group of eminent economists, including several Nobel Prize winners, beginning with Amartya Sen and followed by Joseph Stiglitz (as in the quote above) and Paul Krugman, have criticized the narrow vision, prompted by a superficial quantitativism, of a statistical and economic approach which reduces the situation of any one individual or social category to the level of their income in dollars. Such criticisms are now mutually accepted by both sociologists and economists. It is time therefore to stop targeting economists with unjustified reproaches.

But what, then, is left for the sociologist to say? Let us take things one by one.

When a crisis (and this applies to the current one) splits the economy from the rest of society so that the latter can only focus on its internal problems, what becomes of social life?

It is not only side-lined as a result of the crisis but transformed by it, to the extent even of provoking fear and rebellion against the institutions. Such emotional reactions have, on a number of occasions, nurtured the success of a populist or nationalist authoritarian movement. Take, for example, Hitler's rise to power in 1933, after his movement was bolstered as a result of the 1929 crisis.

At the same time, the crisis accelerates the long-term trend towards a separation between the economic system, including its financial dimension, and the social actors who, as a result of the social crisis, find themselves unemployed, socially excluded or stripped of all their savings, and therefore incapable of reacting politically – the explanation behind the current silence of the victims of the crisis – or transformed into actors who are defined more in universal, moral or cultural terms than social ones.

Conscious of such issues, the sociologist reflects on how the crisis can be overcome. Without rejecting the technical solutions proposed by economists and politicians, the sociologist introduces a new idea. The most important thing, according to him, is to reconstruct society, to end the domination of the economy over society, a process which requires an increasingly general, even universal, principle, to which the term the Rights of Man (more aptly called human rights) can once again be applied. This principle must generate new forms of organization, of education, of governance, in order to bring about a redistribution of the national product in a way that favours work, for so long sacrificed to capital, and to demand a more genuine respect for the dignity of all human beings.

These hypotheses suggest various possibilities in terms of social change, but they exclude any return to the past, to the time prior to the crisis, for any attempt to take refuge in such an illusion would be tantamount to preparing a new crisis.

Sociological analysis differs from that used by economists in that the sociologist, like the historian, seeks to understand the actors, their choices and their social representations. The focus of his or her study is therefore mainly made up of value judgements, even though these must be analysed objectively, with care taken to avoid any ideological bias.

The sociologist seeks to identify the general social and cultural transformations which can be observed in all spheres, through political debates in the first place, but also in writings and images which may not have any obvious connection to current economic problems. The novel and the theatre, the cinema and videos, art, music and songs can thus often provide useful evidence to those studying changes of a general impact.

Of course, the sociologist still needs to turn to the economist in order to learn about the nature and meaning of events. But his main goal must be to link the analysis of the crisis to the context of long-term changes within society. The *key idea* put forward here will be that after the industrial and even the post-industrial society, comes what I call a *post-social situation* (in order to avoid the more obscure term 'post-social society'). Although this process of transformation does not have the same temporality or the same type of consequences as an economic crisis, the two must be examined in relation to each other. Obviously the crisis does not in itself give rise to a new type of society, but it does contribute to the destruction of the old one and it can also prevent a new type of society from developing or favour the intervention of authoritarian actors during a difficult transition period.

Upheavals on this scale, in both the long and short term, can even result in certain actors disappearing altogether. This is the conclusion we must come to when we examine the situation of the trade unions and parties of the 'left' in Europe, now so manifestly impotent that the electors no longer know how to distinguish the left from the right.

The result of this situation was an unexpected silence on the part of society, although this could just as easily be a prelude to the emergence of a violent movement representing all those who have suffered as a result of the crisis. This is the first possible future the crisis could lead to.

But new actors, who can no longer be described as social and who are therefore moral rather than social actors, can also emerge. They uphold the rights of all men against the actions of those who are only concerned with increasing their profits. Clashes between social actors, for example between actors from different 'classes', have been replaced by the glaring contradiction between the economic system, particularly when it focuses exclusively on the quest for the greatest possible profit, and actors who appeal to human rights and respect for all individuals. This second version of the future is as much to be hoped for as the first is to be feared.

Since the beginning of 2010, the 'mega-crisis' seems to have been gradually brought under control and has turned instead into what Paul Krugman refers to as an ordinary depression. But Europe is already in the grip of a serious monetary crisis which brings in its wake a crisis of growth. That being the case, should the sociologist step back in favour of the economists, given that the latter know how to draw up and assess economic policies? Such modesty could be seen as excessive, for the more the economic situation follows a familiar pattern, the more obvious it becomes that the problems associated with it are of a different order from economic forecasts. Here are two examples:

– How will the crisis affect the relationship between the economy and society in the long term?

– Are our societies facing the prospect of a series of crises or are they capable of identifying and constructing a new type of social life, one which I refer to here as the *post-social situ-*

*ation* and which is characterized by the separation between the system and the actors?

One or the other of these two versions of the future will inevitably be ours.

# Part One

## Crises in context

# 1

# Beyond the industrial society

## Economic crisis and changes in society

For many people, the most troubling aspect of the 'mega-crisis' affecting the United States since 2007 and 2008 is its global nature, which has caused the destruction of all the institutions previously responsible for transforming economic situations into elements of a society regulated by the state. Some observers, indeed the majority, regard this as a major crisis of capitalism, which, though not the first, is the worst since that of 1929, with its unforgettable legacy of social destruction. Others refer in apocalyptic tones to the terrifying demise of capitalism and some even talk about the end of the market economy. But, as time goes on, a more measured analysis inevitably takes the place of such immediate deeply pessimistic reactions.

It is not the end of the world. The most pressing concern is the need to evaluate policies of state intervention, particularly those of the American state. For a long time people liked to think that the Washington government allowed its policies to be dictated from New York, that the big business economy set the political direction of this country which dominates the world economy. Today, the vigour of the reactions of the American president and of some major European countries is reassuring, even if it offers no real guarantees for the future. It is all too easy to switch from complete pessimism to blind confidence, even though the states in question have never ceased to be considered as all-powerful, particularly since politics itself has been globalized. An unfounded optimism still emerges sporadically here and there. We hear, for example, talk of an impending end to the current decline or even predictions about the beginnings of a recovery, even if most observers think that any recovery in terms of employment will only manifest itself much later. Other analysts remain more pessimistic and are concerned that the state of crisis is in danger of becoming permanent, dragging the old industrial countries into a decline from which there is no foreseeable way out. But all these predictions end up restricting public opinion to a short-term view based purely on the current economic climate. Of course, this does not mean that economists are wrong to focus their attention on the unfolding crisis, given that public opinion expects to see the success of political interventions, the recovery of the job market and the containment of a climate of insecurity which had initially appeared insurmountable. It is altogether understandable that the public demands forecasts and even prophecies rather than explanations. As though more detailed analyses had no right to be heard until states, banks and businesses had demonstrated the extent to which they could control a situation which, in 2008, appeared uncontrollable.

These observations explain the lack of interest in more wide-ranging analyses, which seem only to furnish us with further reasons to sink deeper into pessimism. Since the 1970s, the so-called neoliberal system seems, moreover, to have come to be identified with contemporary society in all its aspects. This is why the catastrophe is felt more acutely not in the poorest and most vulnerable countries, but on the contrary in the great centres of the global economy such as New York and London. So why look any further?

We need, however, to clearly define what we observe on a daily basis if we wish to strengthen our chances of intervening in a useful way in a global economy we perceive as threatening.

With statistics, particularly American ones, on the state of the domestic market and employment leaving us daily in a state of growing uncertainty or subjecting us to a rapid succession of divergent forecasts, are we in a position to reflect on the nature of the transformations which are taking place? Such reflection is possible, but only by engaging in a debate which is struggling to make headway rather than by simply proffering ready-made solutions. One possible hypothesis is that financial and monetary crises are not in themselves insurmountable, given that others have already been surmounted, provided that states believe in the necessity for them to intervene. But another hypothesis is that we are not simply dealing with a crisis and therefore with an event arising from a particular economic climate, but instead with changes which go beyond the measurable economic facts. Events of such gravity would not only call into question the management of the economy; they would affect the entire organization of our society.

In short, we are in urgent need of a more general analysis, even if we are not in a position to come up with propositions as thoroughly elaborated as those relating to industrial societies, which have the advantage of being the result of several generations of economists. But only by attempting such a task will we be able to formulate policies capable of resolving the current problems.

The justification for this kind of high-risk intellectual undertaking is that the analyses closest to the current economic situation, those we read in the press and on the internet and hear each day on the radio or on television, fail to provide us with results concrete enough to offer us reliable guidance. The triumph of the global free market has been so complete and so entrenched since the 1970s that many people believe it is simply a matter of reconstructing the economy, in all its aspects and with all its determinants. But today, after two years of general crisis and of state interventions in the economy, we know that it is impossible to talk about an economic system in purely economic terms, since state intervention, which has already been given a central role, has demonstrated that the economic system does not govern the whole of society. We therefore have not merely a duty, but an obligation, to situate our analysis on the same level as the economic situation, which has become more political and less exclusively financial. And since we must start by examining the economic situation of the United States, how can we avoid acknowledging that, in this domain, the policies of this country are largely in the hands of President Barack Obama? Conversely, how could we embark on such an analysis without recognizing that in present-day Europe no school of thought or political party currently proposes a convincing vision? Can we, in Europe, speak of a European policy, when the European Union is itself reduced to the role of a minor actor, and when, in the principal European countries, political confusion is at its height? Ideological messages are often so weakened they are in danger of disappearing altogether, leading us to the inevitable conclusion that the lack of robust interpretations of current society is one of the main causes of the crisis. In the light of these two observations, which are both complementary and contradictory, that is to say the subordinate role of economic management with regard to the state and the weakness if not of states, at least of political systems, it seems reasonable to try to understand the interactions between political economy, sociological analysis and even the history of ideas.

For it is only at the most global level, that of the relationships between all types of actors and their capacity to assert themselves, that we can understand the foundations of what is more than simply a succession of economic crises, given that these economic crises have erupted in situations which should be defined in political and sociological terms as much as in economic ones.

### The European model of modernization

In the light of the above comments, it seems appropriate to begin with the definition of the principal concepts underlying the analysis of so-called 'modernized' or 'industrialized' societies.

What has given both our history and our economic, social and political problems their particular character is the fact that, unlike other areas of the world, Western Europe, followed by North America, has refused to see its prime objective as the preservation of the established order, the resistance to factors associated with disintegration and the reinforcement of all systems of control and of the imposition of a comprehensive mode of thought supported by a central power. In the midst of what we call the Middle Ages, both the Arab and the Chinese worlds were better organized, more powerful, and even more efficient and more capable of creative action than a European world which was divided and weakened by the breakup of the Roman Empire and by the lack of real power in societies based on poor communications and the extensive power of the lords, themselves vassals of the feudal system. But the European world abandoned the search for stability and integration, setting itself instead on a completely opposite course, in which all the economic, political, military and scientific resources were concentrated in the hands of an elite, created and legitimized by its powerful domination of the population in every domain. This combination of a powerful elite and a highly dependent workforce created a situation analogous with one in which the maximum amount of energy is produced with the greatest possible potential difference between 'hot' and 'cold' poles, to use the expression of Claude Lévi-Strauss.

This type of society must be defined both by an exceptional capacity in terms of concentration of resources, and by the creation of tensions and conflicts which are always close to the limits of what is tolerable. It is indeed the *polarization* of society which has permitted such a concentration of resources, itself only possible as a result of domination and social exploitation which have existed for several centuries. It is only recently that the dominated have rejected the domination to which they were subjected: nations overthrowing long-standing monarchies, workers fighting to obtain rights, colonies freeing themselves from the colonial yoke and women challenging male domination. Such conflicts have resulted in limits being imposed on those in power, at the risk, however, of weakening investment capacity, as though heralding the end of an era of modernization which had allowed the major Western countries to dominate the world.

The most important thing here is to recognize that this type of society, or rather this type of historical change, is defined both by internal conflicts and by actions directed towards the outside world, usually in the form of conquests. The society we have created has thus been dominated by the opposition between 'masters' and 'slaves', which, beyond the violent conflicts for the most part associated with labour movements, has led to attempts being made to maintain the peace between adversaries without the economy losing any of its dynamism. Various schools of thought have tried to move beyond this opposition between adversaries, in the name of fairness, of justice and of balance. But the significance of these attempts lies more in the fact that they have exposed the central role which conflicts have played for so long rather than in any real progress beyond the central conflict. Nevertheless, we are accustomed (with good reason) to defining Western European society in the second half of the twentieth century as a Welfare State, created as a result of either social-democratic or nationalist policies and by the quest for a new kind of integration. Yet conflict has never disappeared from our societies. From this perspective, there is no complete opposition between an integrated society and a polarized one, given that, in both cases, it is necessary to bear in mind the contradiction between a policy based on accumulation, investment and conquest, and one which supports the claims of the dominated who have increasingly looked for support from a certain conception of the rights and needs of all. This type of society can only function 'normally' if both sides present are clearly defined and if the relationship between them is sufficiently clear to enable politicians to find modes of coexistence (or even of agreement) between them.

This means that the analysis deals with a number of fundamental elements. The first of these is the least well defined in social terms: it involves a certain state of technology, of trade and of resources. So, for example, we all refer to the industrial society or the communication-based society and, when referring to a more distant period, to mercantile capitalism.

From this point on, any description of the situation must be governed by the search for a general analytical principle regarding the actors and their conflicts. If there is no recognized historical context, if no organized and visible economic and social actors have emerged and, finally, if there is no possibility of intervention by a central authority, usually a political one, which tries to resist domination by the richest and to maintain a certain compatibility between opposing interests, we can no longer refer to a type of society.

Which brings us directly to the central question: is there a clear definition of the current issues affecting society, of the dominant and dominated actors, but also of the capacity for institutional intervention, whether by the state or by a parliamentary system?

Yet in our own society it is clear that not only is each of these elements poorly defined, but that they appear to be in the process of breaking down altogether. Which leads to talk of a generalized crisis made up of common issues, the clash of interests and an area of possible state intervention. The world of the dominated has become so diverse and so fragmented that it can no longer give birth to a historically significant actor, or, in other words, to the desire for collective action capable of influencing the path of social progress. The same is true when it comes to those in power. In short, it is difficult to know if there are any institutional systems capable of controlling and guiding both social conflicts and the investment capacity of a society. In many cases, awareness of the contradiction between actors and systems is so pronounced that any potential intervention is rejected in the belief that it is better to leave both dominant and dominated actors to their own devices. Some use the term liberal to refer to a society which claims to be so in economic and political terms, by defining its political dimension in terms of its ability to put in place mediations, or in other words limited agreements. But are we not in reality a very long way from this definition of liberalism, insofar as in the crises we are experiencing, we are no longer capable of defining the equivalent of the fundamental elements of industrial society? It is clear that our current society is no longer one dominated by production and accumulation and by conflicts centred on the appropriation of productivity gains.

But what has replaced all that? Our first objective must therefore be to provide answers to the following questions: what capacity for collective action do the actors possess? Will this take the form of open combat or will it involve agreeing to a certain measure of mediation? And, finally, how can we assess the desire for intervention or non-intervention on the part of political and judicial powers with a view to successfully resolving, by institutional means, the fundamental conflicts?

### The decline of the production-based society

Behind this economic crisis, revealing as it does the fragility of powerful American and English capitalism, it is impossible to ignore the decline of a masculine world based more on money than on machines or products. A hidden but all-powerful world where, as once in the court of kings, splendour rubs shoulders with vice associated not with sex, but with profit disconnected from society as a result of its rejection of all limits and standards.

Creativity has ceased to count. Instead, we see only destruction and impoverishment. Financial capitalism accumulates, producing nothing except a series of 'bubbles' and the poisonous proximity of immense wealth, financial collapse and social crisis. What a distance between the creators of Microsoft and Apple who, almost without money, invented the world of computing or the universe of life, of communication and also of debate which the internet has brought to all areas of human experience and the uncontrolled world of speculation. Techniques which have led to the creation of a civilization in which women in particular seek to reconstruct a human experience which for centuries has been polarized between the conquering elite and the impoverished and subjugated populations. But here too, after so much success and such dramatic progress, the industrial societies find themselves trapped in a dead end, their wealth transferring from the hands of creators and inventors to those of financial speculators.

It would be difficult to make sense of the financial crisis, from which, as always, the speculators are the first to recover, were we not able to glimpse, beyond the present situation, the emergence of a world based on knowledge and also on self-awareness. A creative world, but one completely divorced from a financial economy devoid of utility or reality, which flourished and collapsed, and which those who refuse to mistake the image for the substance must now rise up and control.

The possibility that the world might be destroyed in the relentless search for profit is more than just the symptom of a crisis, since it could sound the death knell for society, starting with free market liberalism, which has destroyed 'capitalist society' by removing all its actors and by reducing it to the rule of the market.

## What kind of society do we live in?

In an industrial society, the transformation of physical resources is clearly the mainspring of society, and conflicts over the distribution of such resources constitute the main source of conflict. Every aspect of social life is defined and sit-uated in relation to this transformation of physical resources and, consequently, by the definition of the actors themselves and of their conflicts in terms of the production of goods and the distribution of any available resources.

Post-industrial society, which is above all a society based on communication, does not differ fundamentally from other stages of industrial society. It is simply (at present) the most advanced manifestation of it. A confusion of ideas has led some commentators to refer to a postmodern society. By this, they mean the disappearance of the central explanatory role given to technological and economic advances, which leads them to affirm the absolute diversity of elements coexisting at any given time.

The real separation of the various conflicts (economic, inter-national, gender) does not signify the absence of any kind of unifying principle but rather the elevation of such a principle to a higher level of universality, that of human rights. The end of the class struggle as the central focus of conflict does not point to a complete fragmentation of society, but instead to the transition, as I have explained, to a new level of unity.

The globalization of the economic system particularly weakens regulatory tools formulated in a national context, and especially the capacity to regulate and control the relationships between economic players by a state capable of both social and economic intervention.

We seem to have reached the end of a long process of de-institutionalization, one which has seen all social categories, their hierarchy, their conflicts and their actors weakened. This sense of the fragmentation and breakdown of elements of the social fabric is as important as was the phenomenon, particularly in the early days of industrialization, whereby individual conflicts were condensed into a more general conflict based on conflicting interests; which incidentally in no way excluded the establishment of forms of regulation and control of social relations and conflicts. We must inevitably reach the conclusion that social actors, in the strictest sense of the term, have declined in importance or even disappeared, but these are being replaced by other non-social actors, in the sense that they bring into play fundamental cultural tendencies.

This phenomenon of the decline of social actors must be seen above all as the consequence of the split between a globalized economy and social conflicts or political actions which are not on a global scale, but which exist on a local or national level. One could even go as far as to claim that once the separation between economic or technological issues and social or political interventions of all types becomes more or less definitive, the notion of *society* becomes meaningless, and even damaging.

Some would immediately object on the grounds that institutions have not ceased to function, at least not in any of the countries in our area of the planet: local transport still operates, dentists still take care of our teeth, and the ritual of the changing of the guard at Buckingham Palace goes on unchanged. If

I use words which seem to ridicule the arguments of those who reject my opinion from the outset, it is because it is all too common to mistake the material functioning of a society for an understanding of the mechanisms which enable an individual or a social category to become actors or, in other words, creators of change. And yet what is worrying is that some people's refusal to acquire a profound understanding of the upheavals our societies have experienced over the course of the last century in fact contributes to their impotence and above all to the growing difficulty individuals and social categories face in seeking to become actors capable of influencing their own history and of controlling or transforming the society in which they live. Of course individuals have always been able to affirm their differences, their own personalities and also some of their opinions, but it is all too easy to see that our society no longer resembles the society described in Marxist manuals half a century ago. Indeed changes have taken place which go in quite the opposite direction to that foreseen by radical groups. The complexity of social relationships has not resulted in a direct conflict between two factions. The very opposite has happened in that there is a growing differentiation between circumstances, categories, groups and opinions. Not that progress has necessarily been made in terms of equality: this is clearly not the case in many countries, including the United States, but simply that the growing abundance of goods and services produced has introduced diversity into the world of consumption, just as it had begun to do in the manufacturing world.

The 'working class' is the best example of this. There is unmistakable evidence of diversification here. We see, for example, an ever widening gap between a central category broadly protected by health and education services and Social Security systems, and a considerable number of categories of socially excluded or marginalized people, so aptly described by Robert Castel as the 'disaffiliated'. Sometimes, within this vast category, small groups are set up, communities form, minority groups challenge the attitudes of the majority – and are even increasingly accepted by them, provided, that is, that they do not seek to overthrow the majority. This situation reflects what many writers have also observed in the context of women's rights. Women are less dependent; both their rights and the differences between the genders are better recognized. But these changes seem to be indicative of very slow progress towards equality between genders, a goal which may indeed never be fully achieved. Some people will certainly refuse to accept such equivocal progress. I have myself found evidence, in the behaviour and opinions of contemporary women, of the emergence of a new collective social and political actor. This opinion remains, however, a minority one. For some, acknowledging pluralisms strengthens the quest for cohesion; for others, on the contrary, there is still substantial evidence of a generalized conflict. Yet all this continues to lead me back to the position I have already described. We do not live in a completely 'fluid' society as Zygmunt Bauman believes, any more than we are part of a generalized social conflict which could manifest itself on any number of 'fronts'. The current century will undoubtedly provide further evidence for all these interpretations. Mass immigration will lead to a mixing of populations which will more often result in conflict than in integration. It will be increasingly tempting to foresee a central conflict in a world split between the West, dominated by the United States, and China with its growing command of markets. And yet the basic principle I have put forward remains valid: the cohesion of movements and of conflicts will take place at an ever more elevated level, one situated far above the strictly social order, at a point where major cultural conceptions assert themselves, influencing behaviour, including social behaviour.

In every domain, social categories are disintegrating and fragmenting. This is most visible in the professional sphere. Between the 'golden boys' and those with little or no job security there is so little common ground that the two can never come into direct conflict. The same is true when it comes to conflicts between the sexes. It is less a case of a conflict between gender categories than a confrontation between the 'polarized' image of society upheld by men and the reintegrated vision of it put forward by women. In each case, we have to move from a social level to a more elevated one, with the result that we are no longer dealing with traditional forms of social conflict but instead with the confrontation between the traditional European model, exacerbated by recent crises, and the stated determination to re-establish links between economic principles and social demands.

Credit should be given to the efforts made by 'socio-economists' to reintegrate the economic and socio-economic aspects of our current situation. Nevertheless, we need above all to recognize the breakdown between these two modes of behaviour and to seek to transform it into a generalized conflict between cultural demands and a vision of a society reduced to purely economic dimensions.

This idea takes us straight to the heart of this analysis in that recent economic crises have generally arisen as the result of a growing divide between the financial economy, often contaminated by the desire for personal enrichment on the part of those in charge, and the 'real' economy, which cannot be defined outside of social conflicts and state interventions.

But this internal breakdown in economic activity also has another significance. For, over and above the rift between financial capitalism and the 'real' economy, looms another, more significant, split between economic activities in general and social, cultural and even political life, accentuated by globalization. Thus, not only is the financial economy separating from the real economy, but economic life as a whole is becoming separated from the rest of society, a situation which threatens to destroy the institutions where the norms and modes of social negotiation are formed. More significant still is the tendency for actors to be defined no longer only in terms of those economic categories which supposedly control social categories. New actors are emerging who no longer correspond to a socio-economic type since they place respect for 'human rights' over a globalization which is beyond the control of any social forces.

This brings us to the central argument of this book: the need to understand how actors are increasingly operating in isolation from the system, and how human experience is both subject to economic necessity and capable of shattering it by setting itself objectives and establishing movements which go against the whole economic system, appealing instead to the human 'subject', to its rights and the laws that protect them.

# 2

# The crisis of capitalist society

In a number of countries, post-war reconstruction paved the way for the creation of major Social Security systems which reduced inequalities within the health sector. But salaries and living conditions had to take a back seat in terms of government priorities. First, it was claimed, priority had to be given to rebuilding all the infrastructures; improvements in living conditions would follow. The first priority was to restore productive capacity, by rebuilding the railway system and by massively increasing the production of cement. Manuel Castells described the lives of French and foreign workers in Dunkirk, lodged in temporary huts where living conditions were difficult whilst working on the construction of high-level technical facilities. The contrast between the grandeur of the finished industrial undertaking and the difficult living and working conditions of the construction workers ended up capturing the public's attention.

Following the decline in state interventionism from the 1970s onwards, another very different rift became apparent. Up until then, senior executives and managers were paid according to their position on a scale based on their qualifications. This situation changed abruptly. The opening of markets and the merging of businesses led to the performance of managers and managing executives being judged on an international scale. And continental Europe soon adopted this model. Over the course of recent years, we have seen the emergence of more and more striking discrepancies between those who are still on a pay scale based on qualifications, and those higher level categories who made sure that their remu-neration, or rather their overall income, was fixed according to their position on the international market. This caused a profound rift between the most highly qualified second-tier managers on the one hand, and on the other, a top tier of managing directors and CEOs operating in the international market as top managers. The very high salaries, bolstered by all sorts of bonuses and other 'golden parachutes', constituted a veritable oligarchy made up of those who generate globalized profits. The current crisis has in particular drawn attention to the case of the *traders*, whose bonuses can sometimes be counted in hundreds of thousands (or even of millions) of euros, and not in thousands (or hundreds) of euros like those of the rest of the workforce. We discovered to our surprise that such benefits were also awarded to managers even when their businesses had not been crowned with success. And it has quickly become clear that it is financial speculation rather than manufacturing products that brings wealth, and that this speculation is responsible for transferring the lion's share of the increased resources into the pockets of a small number of managers, whilst the vast majority of earners continue to battle for increases of 1 or 2 per cent. As a result, executives no longer feel any loyalty to their companies, as is evidenced by a considerable body of research and notably by Olivier Cousin's recent study.

## A second financial sector

We need, however, to look considerably further than the per-sonal enrichment of a small number of people if we are to understand the transformations at work in today's economy. Credit has increasingly outgrown in value the underlying guarantees. A deposit of one hundred dollars in a bank has been transformed into seven hundred dollars placed in hedge funds or, in the construction sector, in subprimes. This imbal-ance has meant that the economy is no longer based on tech-nology and methods of manufacturing and distributing new or improved products, but on the success of operations, the most famous example of which were the attacks directed by George Soros against the pound sterling, which resulted in its devaluation. Certain cases even amount to theft or misappropriation of funds. After the Second World War, industrial leaders invested in reconstruction schemes of both national and social value; over the course of the last few decades, by contrast, capital has been primarily orientated towards speculation. The growing distance between the world of wage-earners and that of managers no longer corresponds to a clash between classes. Instead, internationalization has created a rift between those who have succeeded in becoming part of it and those who cannot hope to do so. At the same time, manufacturing companies were forced to recognize that profits associated with manufacturing were becoming increasingly feeble in comparison with those gained by traders working for the major financial groups.

From the 1990s financial capitalism, increasingly disconnected from the needs of the manufacturing industry, became progressively more and more out of control, though more on a regional scale – in Asia, Mexico, Argentina – than on a global level. Until, that is, the bursting of the new technologies 'bubble' and, above all, the subprime crash which brutally ruined many of those who had resorted to mortgage lenders in order to buy a house.

The United States and the other countries who follow its example, especially within Europe, ascribe little power to those at the forefront of manufacturing, science, education, public health or the arts. Consequently, financial capitalism, encouraged by the American Federal Reserve Bank's policy of low interest rates, under the prolonged presidency of Alan Greenspan, attracted significant amounts of capital to the American market. China, on the other hand, during the same period, increased its savings to 50 per cent of its gross national product, thus enabling the 'State-party' to invest 40 per cent of its GDP.

A great many Americans were consequently caught up in the credit maelstrom. Many private individuals found themselves with debts they could never hope to pay off, while the

American state became heavily in debt to certain countries, and in particular to China, who had acquired a large share of American treasury bonds.

The atmosphere of frenzied consumption which spread through many countries, and in particular the United States, brought de facto support to those leading financiers who were introducing a system of financial operations more risky than the one on which the usual operations of the Stock Exchange was based. Looked at from this perspective, the decline of capitalism, if we can call it that, is due to two main reasons. The first is the one referred to above. Credit transactions, which were both more and more sophisticated and less and less regulated, led to the economic catastrophe of subprimes, but public opinion, though struck by the number of victims, nevertheless failed to mobilize in order to eradicate the root causes of the crisis. The second reason lies in the fact that after a quarter of a century of widespread admiration for the superiority of the neoliberal system, and for American society in particular, American citizens and their European cousins have finally woken up to the weakness and the colossal errors made by the major banks which have led to an exacerbation of inequalities, particularly between the very rich and the very poor.

As a result of economic globalization, much of the world has been contaminated by the new methods of American capitalism with their destructive effects. The 'success' of financial capitalism and the ever-expanding consumer demand led to talk of a crisis of capitalist society (rather than of capitalism), in the sense that the actors of this society have been destroyed (even when its economy still seemed to be functioning satisfactorily).

### The shock and the silence

The collapse of the international banking system, initially an American phenomenon, sent out shockwaves and generated a climate of fear without, however, provoking any major reaction on the part of the victims given that these did not constitute a real social and political group, and that the interests of employees were no more unified than those of the managers, amongst whom, it has been suggested, there were disagreements and conflicts. Initially, when the United States, and in particular the president and the treasury secretary, intervened on a massive scale to prevent the collapse of the banks, American and European public opinion failed to understand why the state, which was manifestly capable of raising so many billion dollars in order to ensure the survival of banks threatened with collapse by the simple expedient of freezing overnight interbank transactions, could continue to oppose very modest salary rises, and, even more, to neglect the victims of the crisis, particularly those affected by the property market. But these interventions resulted in a surfeit of liquidity which still effectively mortgages the future of those countries who have suffered the consequences of the collapse of the banking system.

The majority have finally realized that state participation on a massive scale was indispensable in preventing a systemic catastrophe. However, in certain European countries, such interventions have overturned the rules of the game previously taken for granted by public opinion. As a result, errors made by managers were scarcely sanctioned and the most notorious 'thieves' were allowed to have their slates wiped clean in exchange for light or symbolic sentences, by burying their transgression in the arcane depths of the fiscal system. But Joseph Stiglitz was right to reproach President Obama for not having helped the smaller banks which have a more direct impact on the job market.

This may be the explanation behind one of the most surprising phenomena of our times, notably the silence of the victims, coming as it did at the very time when the economic situation should have aroused reactions that the unions would have been well placed to transform into political protests. No such thing was observed in the majority of countries concerned. The election of Barack Obama can be imputed to a considerable number of factors but certainly not to the existence of a particularly powerful protest campaign, particularly as unions traditionally support the democrat candidate.

And consequently states are today intervening to solve crises they have themselves brought about as a consequence of the excessive trust they put in the wisdom of markets and traders.

Recent developments in the American economic system have had repercussions whose impact has gone far beyond the level of relations between the social actors and the state. Indeed, in the majority of countries the basic elements which played such an important role in industrial societies have virtually disappeared; the decline of the trade unions in particular is almost universal. It is worth remembering here that capitalism refers to a system which is based on a society divided between the elite who control change and receive the profits and those who are trapped inside it with no power to bring about change, a situation which results either in violent clashes, or in the growing 'social-democratization' of states, when they succeed in securing themselves a strong capacity for economic intervention. Capitalism gives a large share of power to leading economic circles, but these are supposed to have a strong awareness of the general interest, and employees can have access to political decisions. Yet this traditional image, which has dominated for so long, now no longer corresponds to reality.

We can indeed no longer define our society in terms of production when the financial markets and their indirect effects on the workings of banks or states have proved so influential. National leaders lost their capacity to act from the moment the economy became broadly 'global', with the result that there is greater proximity between the bankers of London, New York and Tokyo, as Saskia Sassen demonstrated, than there is within any one country between economic leaders and financial leaders who operate according to different criteria, at different speeds and on very different terrains.

These observations lead us to an initial conclusion: we no longer live in a society where social classes contest the distribution of the products of production. And the state acts not so much as an arbiter between the various conflicting social actors than as a mediator between the national economy and its opposite numbers operating on international markets. Amongst those politico-economic actors who until recently occupied an important position within society, few still can claim to do so. For its part, the state in 2010 has almost nothing in common with its 1936 counterpart and with the New Deal. The gravity of the decline in trade unions can be measured against the gap currently existing in Europe between the last countries to recognize strong trade unions – like Italy, Sweden and Germany – and those where they have lost much of their influence. Even the state itself can no longer be seen as a central element in the system of representative democracy. As a result, this is functioning less and less well. The United States has long provided the example of a democratic political system based on a pyramid made up of layers of elections and of decision making which, for better or worse, means that the presidential election is a diluted and extremely indirect expression of public opinion. It is therefore remarkable that the extraordinary success of President Obama cannot be imputed only to the fact that it has put an end to the political exclusion of Afro-Americans, but must also be seen as a massive rejection of the war policies of President George W. Bush. Be that as it may, the social representativeness of the American elections, feeble as it may be, is nevertheless often superior to that of European elections. It was, after all, a British Labour prime minister who allowed the City of London to become a state within a state, and who was responsible for the heavy involvement of Great Britain in the war waged by the United States against Saddam Hussein's Iraq. In Germany, social democracy supported liberal policies. The action of Silvio Berlusconi, former Italian president of the Council, was dictated more by his personal interests than by a political programme, and France elected a right-wing president who was able to include key left-wing figures in his government. And how can we forget the failed attempt to create a Social Security system during Bill Clinton's first presidential term, a failure that President Obama has fortunately, though not without difficulty, managed to redress, thus resolving the disastrous situation of a country which is so advanced in scientific terms and has extremely high levels of resources, but which is nevertheless incapable of ensuring a minimum level of protection to many of its citizens?

Returning to Europe, we observe that the left-wing parties have demonstrated their powerlessness in the face of the crisis, a situation which has led to a weakening in wage claims.

All this evidence of the weakness of the actors in today's society leads us to conclusions which are the opposite of those generally advanced: capitalism has undergone a serious crisis but is emerging from the crisis undiminished, and it is indeed financial capitalism, its active ingredient, which has shown the fastest recovery, even if the near collapse of Dubai, at the end of 2009, cast a passing economic shadow over the major stock exchanges.

### What is a capitalist society?

What lies in ruins are the actors, the modes of dominations, the traditional conflicts and state interventions in the classic sense of the term – in short, classic capitalist society. But it would make no sense to think that a capitalist society is what it is by virtue of being completely dominated by the capitalist economy and the interests of its leaders. For a sociologist, a capitalist society is not merely one with a capitalist economy, since today the China of Mao's successors, like the Russia of Putin and Medvedev, are both capitalist economies, as moreover is the Venezuela of Hugo Chavez.

A capitalist society can only be considered thus insofar as the economic actors in conflict within that society vie for control of the available resources within a *culture* accepted by all and in conditions which allows the *state* to intervene, impelled by the victims of an economic management imposed by capitalist leaders.

This view of the situation, while it may trouble some ideologists, is a widely accepted one, given that social democratic states, who devote a large share of their resources to improving the situation of their populations, are also capable of encouraging their economic leaders to take an extremely active role in international competition. And if certain economic policies, over the course of the last decades, have claimed that there is no longer any place for social actors, by purporting to believe, in accordance with the principles of the *Washington Consensus*, that the rationality of the market should supplant the irrationality of the actors, these claims have finally proved to be laughably misplaced in view of the actual behaviour of financial capitalism and of some of the leaders of industrial capitalism. Today there is a pressing need to once again take account of the non-economic objectives of the economic system, a process which is only possible if the capitalist economy exists within the context of a larger society, made up just as much of anti-capitalist groups and reforming states as of international competitiveness and grasping financiers.

In this way, governments directly address non-economic goals, which are both social and environmental. The major conflicts are no longer centred within a system of production but instead set the globalized economy against the defence of rights which must directly apply to individuals and not only to society.

If it is a question of replacing social actors by moral ones, it is in the hope that, in our reconstructed society, the dominant power of financiers will be limited both by the scope for initiative on the part of industrial leaders as well as those opposed to the non-human principles of a globalized economy and by the interventions of states anxious to stamp out the irrationality of speculative manoeuvres and the spread of social inequalities and unemployment.

The frequently evoked contradiction between a pure economism and the ecologists' concern to save life on the planet must be seen in the same light as that between management and workers in the industrial society. Those who (still) demand the abolition of the capitalist economy would therefore do better to channel their energies into the reconstruction of a capitalist society based on production, given that such a society could not exist unless those defending the workers limit the power of economic and financial actors. Because, as I have pointed out, the most serious aspect of the decline of capitalism is indeed the growing weakness of socio-economic actors and of the interventionist state.

Let us expand the perspective still further. We have become abruptly aware of the extent to which we had distanced ourselves from the problems associated with production, and deprived of those advantages of capitalism associated with the major technological and scientific discoveries, which have enabled many people to live longer and ensured the protection of that those rejected by society. Alive, creative, riddled with tensions and conflicts, this society has become almost unreal, so dense is the smoke-screen of lies and secrets that has locked us into the world of the present moment. In this world, human beings have lost the capacity to be who they want to be and to defend their fundamental rights.

# 3

# The crisis situation

## The financial hurricane

We are not used to dealing with phenomena on such a scale. Many businesses find themselves paralysed by the financial crisis, a crisis which cannot be contained or resolved except by the injection into the economy of liquidity in amounts far exceeding their means.

The current crisis was preceded by a number of others which, though on a smaller scale, nevertheless indicated the fragility of the financial system. In 1990, for example, the 'Savings & Loans' crisis affecting American savings banks played an important role in the 1991–2 recession. In 1995, the sensational fall of Barings Bank in Great Britain and then, in 1998, the collapse of certain hedge funds heralded the impending storm. Following the bursting of the high-tech bubble in 2001 and the Enron scandal (31 October 2001), the collapse of the Amaranth fund and then, from 2007 onwards, the American subprime crisis, led to a generalized crisis. It was the fall of Lehman Brothers on 15 September 2008 that triggered the catastrophe.

These crises, coming in the wake of those which had erupted during the preceding decade in Asia and Latin America, and following the freeze in the Japanese economy, originated more often than not from dangerous financial initiatives and quickly assumed gigantic proportions. The proliferation of derivatives and of securitization, that is to say, the process through which debts held by the banks are transformed into bonds or other types of securities, put 600,000 billion dollars into circulation in 2007 – that is to say 12 times the world GDP.[1] The real estate bubble, though on a smaller scale, still accounted for 30,000 billion dollars. In Great Britain, the City, the most important stock market in the world, represents a growing share of GDP. These vast financial universes far exceed their true base, defined in terms of economic guarantees.

Certain countries are particularly badly affected: Spain with debts reaching 160 per cent of disposable income; Great Britain, where the level is 140 per cent; the United States, with 130 per cent. In social terms, the key factor is the rise in inequality, especially in the United States, and, even more importantly, the dramatic rise in the incomes of top managers, which during this period went from 40 to 400 times the salary of the average worker.

Equally significant are the transformations affecting the world economic order during the same period. The first, and most obvious, involves the increasingly significant role of the major emerging countries – the BRIC countries: Brazil, Russia, India and China. World trade is re-organizing itself around these countries: their exports of raw materials, particularly agricultural goods, now supply both the industrial and high-tech industries of the Northern countries. Some of them, led by China, are developing high-quality industrial production. The Northern hemisphere countries no longer control the global context, even if they still retain a quasi monopoly in terms of research, development and generation of capital. The G8 countries have in fact been replaced by the G20, which is opening its doors to emerging countries, but at the same time there is talk of a G2 – the United States/China – which would have a huge capacity for decision making and for negotiation, even if China refutes this notion. Europe has been seriously weakened by all these changes. And the economy of the Northern hemisphere,

[1] Global GDP at that time was 50,000 billion dollars. In the United States, it amounted to 11,000 billion dollars and in France 2,000 billion dollars.

in particular that of the United States, is subject to severe imbalances.

It required a strong initiative on the part of the United States and the Paulson plan of 700 billion dollars of liquidity injected into banks and major businesses, along with the 636 billion proposed by the British government, the 480 billion from Germany, the 360 from France (partly in the form of guarantees), plus the smaller contributions from other countries, to prevent the collapse of the world economy. A success so brilliant it would quickly encourage banks in America and elsewhere to resume their favourite pastime, speculation, just as soon as their debts were paid.

Over and above this quantitative evidence, the most significant change worth pointing out is the fall of the executives and senior managers, whose influence within companies had been hailed by John K. Galbraith. In effect, the new bankers, far from taking responsibility for economic development, effectively caused the collapse of the banking system. In other words, financial considerations, hitherto regarded as the triumph of economic rationality, ended up being subverted by banks intent on pursuing increased profits and even the personal enrichment of their managers, as demonstrated by a number of major scandals (one of the most striking being the 50 billion dollars accumulated by Bernard L. Madoff, former head of the Nasdaq).

This major crisis marks the end, the final death knell of the neoliberal era which, from the mid-1970s, had replaced the managed economy introduced after the war, at a time when only governments could command the means required to get the old industrial countries back on their feet and to launch the economies of the de-colonized countries.

The crisis not only affects the management and governance of the economic world; it comes just as culture and its values are in the throes of a radical transformation, characterized by a less intense focus on work, and the declared desire, particularly amongst young people, to have experiences of a personal nature rather than simply participating in often depersonalized collective tasks, as well as by the development of new methods of communication in the digital age.

But, even more importantly, as we move towards a new type of society and a new economy, comes the realization that we are rapidly approaching limits which cannot be exceeded without putting our very existence on Planet Earth in mortal danger.

Of course, the split between the financial economy and the real economy, which organizes the production and distribution of goods and services in response to demand, is not a new phenomenon, and crises arising as a result of such a split have at various times affected the progress of production and productivity in different economic situations. But what makes the current crisis exceptionally serious is the fact that the financial world has been split in two. The banks have created a financial world outside the reach of their own rules and control systems. And it is these derivatives that have engulfed the hedge funds and subprimes.

### Experts and governments

Two complementary reasons justify turning to sociology in a field of study dominated by economics: firstly, the absence (or insignificance) of sociological considerations in the analyses put forward by the vast majority of economists; secondly, the fact that the sociological approach is the only one capable of throwing light on certain aspects of the current crisis.

The question of the failure of economic thought, or at least of its mainstream, has been robustly examined by Paul Krugman and Joseph Stiglitz and in a more detailed way by Norberto E. García, in his book, *La crisis de la macroeconomía*, published in 2010. The central concept championed by these authors, and by a number of others, is that the reason for this failure lies largely in the predominance of a method of analysis so widely accepted as the classic approach, it had to be given precedence over any others. Thus, in the wake of the violent rejection of the Keynesian school of thought in the United States, we saw the emergence of an alliance amounting almost to a fusion between the neo-classicists and the neo-neo-Keynesians. This newly dominant school of

thought was built around classic and fundamental principles, such as the hypothesis of rational behaviour on the part
of actors in seeking their own interests and the construction
of a general equilibrium based on bringing these rational actors
together, and, taken to its logical conclusion, the capacity of the
market to re-establish its internal balance when this is threatened. No doubt this school of thought simply reflects, in economic terms, American hegemony over the world, following
its victory over the Soviet system at the end of a long cold war.
From this perspective, this trend in economic thinking could
therefore be considered as the ideological expression of this
hegemony, particularly given the fact that it offers no scope
for the consideration of social or political players, rejected by
the model of the rational economic player. This ideology was
not, however, equally dominant in all the centres of economic
research. Paul Krugman thus humorously pitted the fresh-water
economists working in the area of the Great Lakes, and particularly in Chicago, against the salt-water economists, including both those based on the East Coast at Harvard, MIT, Yale,
Columbia and Princeton and their West Coast colleagues based
primarily at Berkeley and UCLA. But any opposition between
them is limited in scope and should not be interpreted as the
expression of a conflict between two giants. Few economists,
even on the two coasts, anticipated the mechanisms which led
to the crisis we are now familiar with or were capable of fore-
casting it. Joseph Stiglitz and Paul Krugman were amongst the
principal 'non-conformists' (which was no obstacle to both of
them being awarded the Nobel Prize).

The dominant American ideology was, from this point of
view, a restrictive reality, put together under several presi-
dents, and in particular, by Ronald Reagan. Nor did Bill
Clinton's presidency do anything to change the situation.

Clearly it is not a matter of seeking to identify the origin
of the crisis in the silence of the majority of economists. To
do so would both overestimate the influence of academic
economists and underestimate that of banking and business
leaders. But since the current crisis is based on a breakdown
in the relationship between the financial economy and all
other sectors of society, it seems logical to emphasize that

this silence and its negative consequences are an inseparable element in the decline of the Western world at a global level, and in particular in the ending of the hegemony of the United States; which does not of course imply that they have lost their superiority in every area. The situation was no different in Europe, where the contribution to economic thought was, throughout this entire period, nevertheless considerably weaker than that of the Americans, with the (traditional) exception of Great Britain and notably of the Cambridge school, heirs to the Keynesian tradition.

For any sociologist, an economic crisis (and in particular a financial one) signals above all a breakdown and perhaps the decay of a society defined as a social ensemble where the interplay of domination or of conflicts, which can sometimes result in violent clashes, is usually, and especially in so-called democratic societies, limited because both sides have the same view of society and share the same ideals in terms of behaviour and of institutions. The case of industrial society is clearcut: management and employees who were the main actors in any conflicts shared broadly the same vision of the economic world: they all attached positive value to work, to production and above all to growth in productivity which generates higher salaries and an increased sense of well-being. Moreover, governments, either directly or under pressure from political forces and the unions, constantly intervened in social conflicts, in particular in social democratic countries, in support of the workforce or of those temporarily or permanently excluded from the world of work. The two main objectives of the state are therefore to reduce inequality and to provide maximum security to the workforce. In France, a third of household incomes comes from measures taken to redistribute wealth and to protect the workers, a situation which has had positive consequences in terms of reducing the share of national income directly affected by the financial and economic crisis.

The crisis in itself is not dealt with and resolved by the victory of one social group over another. Moreover, crises always generate an increase in inequality, as was the case in the United States recently, and this makes interventions with a social or political objective all the more urgent (and all the more difficult). The reconstruction of society, by means of state intervention and under the influence of a common conception of society shared by the actors in a conflict, is the best way of curbing the crisis.

Our current society is characterized by the fact that massive state interventions have meant that the banks have seen a rapid recovery in profits, while unemployment rates are set to remain high long after the economy starts to recover. In the immediate aftermath of the collapse of Lehman Brothers, state intervention thus avoided a catastrophe, but it did not succeed in rebuilding the socio-economic system, and even President Obama was unable to impose on the banks the reforms he considered indispensable.

It is worth noting on this subject that although economists are right to identify the surfeit of liquidity and the general debt levels in the United States, from the state to individuals, as the deep-seated reasons for the crisis, it nevertheless remains that the behaviour of the very rich, driven by the search for maximum profit, was, and continues to be, the prime factor in the breakdown of the social system – that is to say of any possibility of either the state or the workforce intervening in the working of the economy.

Since 2011, and particularly in Europe, the inability of governments to control financial capital, serious as the consequences were, is no longer the most significant and dramatic aspect of the failure of governments. At the very moment when a recovery of the financial system began to seem possible once again, it became clear that a number of European countries were in desperate straits and on the brink of bankruptcy. Iceland and Ireland had suffered severely as a result of the financial crisis, but it was in Greece first of all, and then in Portugal, and subsequently across the entire Eurozone, that the threat of a new catastrophe began to emerge. In order to avoid a general economic crisis provoked by falling consumption, the European countries – plus the United States in this case – had accumulated debts on a hitherto unknown scale. In a number of countries, public debt amounted to more than 100 per cent of GDP. The most vulnerable countries, such as Greece and Portugal, could no longer borrow at the prohibitive rates which were driving them into bankruptcy. Those states which had successfully urged the adoption by all members of the European Union of a code of good behaviour, prohibiting countries from exceeding budget deficits of more than 3 per cent, now found themselves forced to go well beyond this level. This was particularly the case in France, which had been particularly adamant about the necessity of respecting the 3 per cent deficit limit.

The United States had few concerns about their external debts since American Treasury bonds were selling very well, particularly in China, Japan and Brazil and because military spending, in Iraq and in Afghanistan, appeared to correspond to a national imperative, as President George W. Bush, the principal decision maker on military involvement in Iraq – along with the British prime minister – was quick to point out.

The decision taken in mid-2011 by the ratings agency *Standard & Poor's* to downgrade American debt from triple A to AA did not induce the panic some had feared, given that the robustness and creativity of the American economy continues to guarantee the United States an economic leadership which China, in spite of its very strong growth, cannot rival.

But in Europe the situation is very different. Great Britain, a financial giant, has for a long time been in the throes of the crisis of deindustrialization affecting almost all the European countries, with the exception of Germany, which has managed to sustain its heavy industry within its borders and which supplies machine tools and cars to the major emerging countries. Spain, after a period of enormous prosperity almost entirely due to the very strong growth of the construction industry, itself closely linked to tourism, plunged into a serious economic crisis which saw unemployment rates rising to over 20 per cent. Nevertheless, the Spanish economy is protected by virtue of its very size, since the measures involved in its rescue appear to go beyond anything the other Eurozone countries would be prepared to envisage. The solidarity between members of this zone is seriously undermined and Germany, in particular, only belatedly agreed to participate in the rescue of Greece.

But in the wake of first the financial and then the monetary crisis, a third crisis, the least spectacular but the most serious, is gradually emerging: the crisis of growth. Here in Europe, Italy is the worst affected with an average growth of only 0.1 per cent over the ten-year period 2001–11. But many other countries are not far off this disturbing result. Germany itself only achieved 0.5 per cent growth on average during this period. In contrast with the United States, whose economy seems remarkably healthy, Europe seems incapable of growth.

The sociological reasons behind the growth crisis are even more important than in the case of the previous crises. A surprising case is that of France, one of the countries in the world where the inhabitants have the most negative views of themselves and of their leaders, in spite of the fact that their country, though mediocre, is one of the least badly placed within the Eurozone. This is evidence of a lack of self-confidence which can be put down to contradictions in terms of self-perception. Such contradictions, which are equally present on both the left and the right, make it impossible to predict how the political future of France will develop in the short term. It would be interesting to find out why the Italians, although in a worse situation, have a much more positive image of themselves, in spite of the fact that Silvio Berlusconi, the dominant figure in Italian life for more than a decade, is the target of very serious criticism from both inside and outside his country.

From the beginning of 2007 until the end of 2011, the sociological and political aspects of crises have taken on ever greater weight, to the extent that economic solutions are generally met with negative reactions as demonstrated by the Italian budget reform plans.

## Beyond manufacturing societies

The coming together of two movements, one tending towards the domination of the financial economy and the other toward changes in manufacturing methods, means that the internal problems of businesses seem less important in the light of the financial crisis and the resulting unemployment, and of the transformations in the world economy. At the highest level, we are primarily preoccupied today by the threat posed to our survival by an uncontrolled economy. We have moved from technological growth to a realization of the serious threats imposed by the acceleration of the greenhouse effect, the injection into the atmosphere of ever increasing amounts of carbon dioxide, the flood risks affecting vast coastal areas as a result of melting glaciers – even if this is happening at a slower rate than predicted – and, more generally, by the rise in temperatures and the consequent shift in climate zones. All of which has led us to wonder whether the time has come to abandon a mode of production and of managing resources which had hitherto been synonymous with progress. By the same process, environmental politics has acquired an importance equal to that of economic politics, and it has become obvious that any such transformation could only be successful if decisions were agreed on a global level, and if consumption levels were reduced – both in the rich countries and in the newly emerging countries, particularly China – to a level compatible with the increase of resources in the poorest countries.

We need to abandon our tendency to identify technical innovations not only as the main cause of social and even political change, but also as the solution to under-development or to situations where development is frozen. Contradictions multiply as we move away from policies decided on a national level, given that problems are increasingly globalized. Not that this makes them any easier to resolve, as the recent failure of the Copenhagen climate conference clearly demonstrates.

From now on we need to control production and consumption by taking into account the needs and possibilities of all categories of people living on the planet. Yet how can we agree on decisions which are compatible with both the growth of poor countries and with the reduction in the negative consequences associated with the lifestyle of the richer ones? Since the world-wide summits in Rio, Kyoto and Doha, we have come to the conclusion that all countries, including the United States, should be subject to international decisions. And the current crisis is an opportunity to reflect on how all these imperatives can be balanced: is there a need for generalized change?

There are links between the reliance of businesses on financial markets and that of individuals reduced to being no more than consumers dominated by what the market offers. As a result, the triumph of the financial economy has ended up affecting every aspect of personal and collective life. The reliance on advertising and on pricing policies is increasingly directly felt by the majority of people, who are both attracted and overwhelmed by these campaigns. Given that workers are no longer at liberty to choose their jobs, many of them find themselves confronted with new problems which they are incapable of dealing with or resolving. Suicides, withdrawal, mental illnesses all point to the fact that individuals feel increasingly crushed by a system which ostensibly gives them increased responsibility and freedom, but which exposes them more and more to the strategies of companies and markets. All of which is in contradiction to the ideology of 'human relations' which set out to reconcile the economy with the needs of the individual.

It is clear that vulnerable workers are being increasingly exposed by the management to attacks from the markets, and that companies increasingly focus on protecting themselves from passing storms, leaving their front line workers to take the brunt of these, regardless of their place in the hierarchy. Companies are conscious of their inadequate capacity to influence changes which affect them directly. And if the biggest businesses sometimes display considerable optimism, in the sense that they see themselves as being protected by the state, small and medium sized companies are acutely aware of their diminishing power. They do their best to 'run a tight ship', in other words by imposing tight controls on every aspect of their operation. The 'humanist' stance, in vogue immediately after the war, has consequently almost disappeared, insofar as its grand declarations no longer have any influence on decisions taken or on the problems to be solved.

All of which supports the hypothesis already put forward here, namely that, looking beyond the crash, the crisis essentially represents a transformation on a greater scale than any we have encountered in the past, in that it is not simply a matter of technological modifications, but also of new social relationships which expose workers increasingly directly to the stress induced by direct market pressure. It is therefore no longer 'sound management' of a business which counts, since it will, in any case, have to submit to the demands of the market. At the same time, the old notion of technological determinism has disappeared. Research aimed at boosting productivity is still important of course, but to a secondary degree. More important is the capacity of a business to face the challenges of an unpredictable market.

A business used to be essentially a collection of machines and a budget; today it has become a system confronted with many different dangers, particularly of a financial nature.

This challenge to the notion of an industrial society, centred on the company and its voluntarism to act freely, has been overtaken by another one. Many books and commentators have claimed that the concept of work is out-dated, that from now on our societies will be based instead on research and communication. A few even dare to speak of a society based purely on leisure and predict the demise of the workforce. The notion that work is the noblest form of activity and the one most apt to produce high-quality human beings should no longer be taken at face value. Such a notion serves only to restore to favour the optimistic vision of Western capitalism. The collapse of the USSR and its associated 'democratic republics' encourages celebration in those Western countries who, long before others, managed to increase their production and their productivity, and by doing so improved the working and living conditions of their employees. And yet it is clear that if work has not diminished in importance in our lives, the destiny of our societies, in the immediate future, is more directly threatened by crises affecting the financial system than by the working conditions of employees. These are the principal victims and it is impossible to imagine that the solution to the crisis will lie in a return to worker power and to the strains of a permanent hymn in praise of work and the workers.

# 4

# The breakdown of society

## The demise of conscience

We need to make a distinction between the history of a financial and economic crisis and the transformation which causes
us to move from one type of society to another, as was the
case with the shift from a preindustrial society to an industrial one in Great Britain in the eighteenth century and in
Belgium, France and other countries in the mid-nineteenth
century. It is in the context of a transformation on a similar
scale that our hypotheses need to be formulated. Such a
stance seemingly distances us from the questions which fas-
cinate the majority of observers and the public: will we come
through the crisis? How many years will it take? At what
cost? No one today can provide a definitive answer to any of
these questions. Nevertheless, over the last two years, it has
become clear that a generalized collapse has not occurred
and also that the election of Barack Obama has raised our
hopes for positive change. It is true that the collapse of the
Greek economy in February–May 2010, the first indication
of a generalized monetary crisis, represented a serious threat
to Europe, which was nevertheless able to deal with it. In
a crisis, as in a hurricane, the intentions and aims of those
caught up in the storm are of little significance. When a new
society is in the process of being created however, it is a different matter.

We are already half way there: the past is receding and we are leaving it behind us. We are therefore in a better position to examine in more detail the shape of the world to come.

We have come a long way from an economic model in crisis: we no longer hear the praises of neoliberalism being sung and it has lost much of its glory. We discovered to our horror that a large number of top executives had behaved like thieves – or swindlers. The reputation of those in charge of banks and major companies, particularly in the United States, has, in the space of a very few years, been turned on its head. This does not, of course, imply that all of them are equally tarnished. Over the course of a few months (or a few years), it was as though the market, in which liberalism placed its full confidence, had been transformed into a multiplicity of decision-making centres, many of which were hidden from public view. And even today the largest banks continue to protect their own interests, in spite of the strong reactions of a public still reeling from the effects of the crisis.

The neoliberals tried to make us believe that we were all subject to the laws of economics, that we would not be able to gain control of the economic situation, and still less free ourselves from 'structural' realities. Yet it is these champions of economic determinism themselves who now appear to be primarily responsible for a crisis they have to a large extent provoked and fuelled, ignoring, for the sake of their own predominantly personal interests, the needs of businesses and companies locked in a permanent struggle for survival. The financial economy has become detached from the real economy and the latter has severed its links to a society of which it should be an integral part. Until recently, it was rare to hear mention of trillions of dollars or of euros. And yet it has required interventions on this scale to enable currencies, frozen by an atmosphere of fear, to circulate once again in and between banks. But we are all too aware that it is not enough to blame a handful of people at the top. Even if certain individuals are highly significant, in particular those in government, and even if public opinion turns out not to be very influential after all, given that it comes too late, it is nevertheless still possible, as Keynes discovered, for governments to rebuild what has been destroyed or severely shaken up as a result of the actions of a handful of adventurers and of a few hundred traders, paid in hundreds of thousands of euros. These simple comments support the hypothesis that it would be dangerous to focus our attention on the consequences of the crisis, and on how to recover from it, when what we are experiencing weakens society as a whole, turning it into a victim of the financiers. This is why there is an urgent need to come up with new types of analysis: just as the crisis itself is a theatre without actors, so the way out of the crisis and the formation of a new society will depend on initiatives either taken by governments or imposed by the victims themselves.

### The silence of the political parties and of the unions

How is it that in our well-informed and democratic countries, the rumblings of thunder which preceded the major crisis went unheard? Why, when industrial crises, company closures or re-locations had for years provoked reactions of anxiety and anger, some of which were extremely violent, was the alarm not sounded? Clearly it is not enough to blame political parties and governments; it is also necessary to question the mechanisms which prevented both militants and observers from gaining a clear understanding of the situation and taking action. Take the case of Italy. The crisis within the left, the Partito Democratico (PD), a crisis which may yet become more serious still, means there is little chance of any political awakening in Italy. The extreme-left in Europe, whether of communist origin or, as in the case of Die Linke ('the left'), formed as a result of a split in the German social democrat party and strengthened by the former Communist Party of Soviet-dominated East Germany, are vociferous and even violent in their criticism, but lack the force to intervene. The unions continue to lose ground and still no system of protection against the crisis has been put forward.

The principal reason behind the weakness of European political parties is that having believed in the philosophy of progress, with its emphasis on voluntarism, and even idealism, they then abandoned it following the First World War and the Soviet revolution. Attention was focused instead on the inevitable crisis of capitalism which could only be overcome by revolutionary action, giving new meaning to the concept of progress. This was clearly evoked by the young Georges Friedmann in *La Crise du Progrès*, written when he was still closely associated with the Communist Party. In France, the role to be played by the leading union was not chosen; it was imposed by the Communist Party, itself conforming to the party line laid down by Moscow. Many intellectuals subscribed, more or less enduringly, to this dramatic vision which subjected men to the edicts or *ukases* of the Party. The USSR had emerged victorious from the war against Nazi Germany; it imposed its will on half of Europe, resulting, in the remaining half, in a repression against the Communist Party which varied in strength depending on the individual countries. And the Communist Party drew a considerable part of its prestige from this. The second half of the twentieth century, up until 1989, was therefore dominated by ambivalence on the part of intellectuals towards the notion of communism. They claimed to remain faithful to the revolutionary ideal but, since this could not be achieved, they retreated instead into systematic criticism of the Western world, leading to violent attacks against its idealism, which, according to them, masked the omnipresence of oppression exercised by the dominant class.

Unable to eliminate capitalism and the United States, they chose as their target the very notion of the *subject* accused of every conceivable crime. This alibi for revolutionary action effectively destroyed political action, within a democratic framework severely weakened by the presence of the predominant communist model, right up to the end of François Mitterrand's first term of office. Hence the enthusiastic support of students and teachers for a Trotskyism which they reinterpreted in an arbitrary manner, and then for social philosophies such as that formulated by Pierre Bourdieu, whose notion of *habitus* leaves only limited scope for any initiative on the part of actors. Philosophers took advantage of this situation to side-line sociologists, who, for their part, rejected the notion that actors could be eliminated.

When the crisis threatened and then erupted, the forces which had been associated with the revolutionary movement after 1917 had already been reduced to silence. This was particularly noticeable in the aftermath of 1968, and after worker-led management had finally burnt itself out in 1973 in the Lip factory. The workers of the Lip factory were the last to support the establishment of a non-capitalist company motivated by the quest, partly a Christian one, for a revolutionary subject. The collapse of this old model was even more dramatic in Italy where, after several demonstrations organized in protest against companies and their management, terrorism took control of those organizations closest to the revolutionary model, leading to the 'dark years', marked by bombings and finally the assassination of Aldo Moro, the Christian Democrat who had taken it into his head to come to an agreement with the communists.

Again after 1989 and the fall of the Berlin Wall, and especially at the time of the general strike of 1995, the weakened state of revolutionary capacity in France was evident, in spite of the calls to action put out by *Le Monde Diplomatique* and by Pierre Bourdieu. The fear of losing one's job in no way explains the feeble nature of any demonstrations or criticism. Post-communist intellectuals had exerted too great an influence. Those who opposed them were unable to act, marginalized to the point of paralysis, and incapable of defeating an ideology that rendered action impossible. The economic and social disaster of 2007–9, the effects of which will continue to be felt for a long time to come, saw the situation deteriorate still further, against the background of almost complete silence on the part both of intellectuals and militants. In other words, unless backed up by a revolutionary party or capable of bringing about reforms, extreme intellectual opposition will generate only silence and impotence.

## The responsibility of intellectuals

Such observations, indisputable as they are, nevertheless fall short of explaining the silence and helplessness of the victims and their political representatives. In the current crisis, observers have undoubtedly been particularly struck by the absence of reaction to the reduced share of national income taken by wage earners. But how can such a failure of social democracy be explained? The counter-example of the Scandinavian countries demonstrates that this decline of social democracy was not inevitable, and suggests that it was undoubtedly caused more by political than economic reasons – a theory which is backed up by the arguments of some social democrat leaders, like Michel Rocard in France, who was adamant that the increasingly obvious weakness of social democracy was largely the result of its inability to rise to the defence of workers. His argument is sound, but the issue still remains: how can this weakness be explained? Certainly not through the mistakes and whims of any individual leader, such as Guy Mollet in France, who had no scruples in taking control of the struggle against the FLN (National Liberation Front) in Algeria.

This observation fails to bring any solution to the current crisis since it merely throws light on the background to the failure by the main social and political forces stemming from an industrial society to maintain their capacity to act in today's society. It is clear that if we wish to exert any influence over the world currently taking shape, we will need to understand that sustainable development can only be achieved through deliberate action, with the attendant understanding that we need to place our hopes not in the reconstruction of the past, but in our capacity to create a new world.

This task is no more or less difficult than was that of overthrowing monarchies, challenging industrial power or recognizing the right to be different. And to achieve it we must first learn to see things from a different point of view and understand the developments which, though they cannot resolve the crisis, will bring about long-term changes.

## The universal and the particular

In order to enter this new world, we need to identify the factors which determine, on the one hand, a collective awareness of being part of the same historical moment, and, on the other, the determination of each individual to stand up for their own identity, and therefore their difference. This is a theme familiar to sociologists, who for a long time were split into two separate camps over the question. On one side were those who believed in the universalism of the Age of Enlightenment, and, on the other, those who, on the contrary, sought for recognition of the particularity, the specificity of each human group in relation to each other. We are only now discovering – albeit belatedly – that the particular and the universal are by no means incompatible.

We have already entered a world in which we are all equal but at the same time different. From the moment the skies cleared and the prophecies made by politicians had all been proved false, we became aware that we had invented an image of ourselves which allowed us to take action in a world where the rights of individuals would be universally recognized. And at the very moment when some people thought a human point of view was redundant, we found ourselves entering a world where action impacts on an environment we have created ourselves. Today it is within this world, shaped by our plans, our conflicts and our negotiations, that the universality of our condition as human beings endowed with the same rights, establishes itself. This creation of a world on a 'human' scale clashes with the violence and contempt of empires, but it asserts the rights of everyone, rights which are universal in that they are independent of fortune, of political power, of religious authority or of family status. (Which does not mean that all human beings have become equal but that they are more clearly aware than in the past of the common ground that exists between individuals and groups with different functions, operating in very different social spheres.) The powerful, the poor, illegal immigrants, all live in separate worlds, but have the same 'equal rights', an equality proclaimed by the teachings of Christ as set down in the Gospels, but present too in other religions as well as in the philosophy of the Enlightenment through the concept of secularism.

In short, the human space we now occupy implies a demand for equality which is continually extending the right to life to all social categories on the planet, as is evident from the sympathetic response of the vast majority of people to the humanitarian battles waged by those who refuse to accept the inequalities into which some people are born and which persist throughout their lives.

Reconciling equality and difference is no easy task, but it is at the very heart of our beliefs and is beginning to have a major influence on our behaviours, particularly in a social context.

## Is the end of society imminent?

It is true that in past centuries, in the absence of sociologists, writers and journalists took it upon themselves to expose the extent of child poverty and destitution, the brutality of their employers and indeed of their fathers, the vast numbers of paedophile crimes going unpunished, etc. Improvements in the living standards of the majority of people in certain countries have contributed to a reduction in such suffering, but the thirst for consumption has driven the poor to consign the very poor to a position of abject inferiority in order to draw a distinction between them. If it has become difficult, or even impossible, to refer to social classes, it is not because social and professional relationships are more relaxed, but because the major social categories have fragmented into smaller groups, which has led not only to a differentiation between such groups but also to conflicting behaviours. Certain categories in particular, such as immigrant workers, find themselves rejected by a proportion of the population.

All of this should encourage a certain mistrust of the vocabulary of the nineteenth century and of the leaders of the first workers' organizations. What can qualified workers, many of whom have indeed become technicians, have in common with unqualified workers hit by unemployment and with the growing numbers of those who are socially excluded and unable to find regular work? The latter category almost always accounts for 15 per cent of the workforce in industrialized countries, and when the employment market is hit by crises like the current one, this figure rapidly rises to 18 or 20 per cent of the population. Between these categories there is enormous diversity, making it therefore impossible to represent society in terms of a pyramid where each layer has its own distinctive characteristics. Barely half a century since the period of reconstruction following the Second World War, the economic crisis, the rise in unemployment, the inadequacies of both general and vocational education have turned society into a wasteland blighted by poverty and helplessness, spreading to the very heart of many political systems, both left and right.

*Society no longer exists.* If this phrase, which has been on my lips for so long, is easier to understand now, it is because the differences and connections between the various groups no longer allow us to distinguish those broader categories hitherto referred to as social classes which corresponded to specific lifestyles and social relationships. We need therefore to find other means of classifying the observable facts, which will enable us to take into account both the positive and the negative elements which are evident at every level of society. Over the last 20 years, we have focused less on the triumphant rise of executives and more on their fall, as their techno-economic skills were crushed by the massive power of money and, in the United States at least, by rising inequality. Changes have happened so rapidly that even those categories which seemed the most stable, the so-called professions, now extending beyond the traditional ones (doctors, teachers, lawyers, company executives and even top management), find themselves in free fall, as evidenced in France by the dissatisfaction and the increasingly frequent and radical demonstrations organized by teachers, hospital staff and many public sector workers. While we must acknowledge that the constraints imposed by power, customs and beliefs have been weakened or have disappeared, we are nevertheless forced to accept the validity of many of the complaints put forward by those in favour of the old regime when they denounce violence, the break-up of the family, psychological crises, rising rates of both serious and petty crime, ranging from 'disre-spect' to armed robbery and murder. The loosening of social bonds makes us feel we are caught up in a whirlwind from which there is no escape.

It is no longer a matter of choosing between the prospect of freedom obtained by means of a struggle and this insecu-rity which paves the way for repression. Instead we need a new set of criteria on which to base our judgement.

The need for money dominates those, and they are many, who live under the shadow of unemployment or poverty. But all of us, whether employed or on the fringes of society, are victims of a lack of communication – or even of intimacy. We delight in contrasting the quality of intimate relationships and a taste for weighty cultural works with this 'mass culture' so long referred to in scathing tones, in comparison with so-called 'high culture'. Those who think along these lines fail to understand the world we live in, for their imagination is peopled more by characters from films or the theatre than by close or more distant relatives, casual acquaintances or old school friends. Yet it is exactly such experiences that allow us to come into contact with the greatest number of people, to discover what is in fact the opposite of a social type, in other words, this cast of characters which enables us to iden-tify the human subject within ourselves. As a result, what takes the place of the hierarchy on which the old world was based is the capacity (present or absent) of each individual to respect the subject in themselves and in others. The romantic hero has often been portrayed as someone who claims to have broken free from the limits of the forbidden but who, because of his weakness, must eventually find himself cross-ing the social or geographic barriers which set the strength of the group against the frailty of the individual. But these very words give too easy a victory to the collective norms. Today it is through individual experience that we can identify those who are best able to help us understand ourselves, and to make us better able to discover the Other.

The rapid expansion of mass culture, so it is said, leads to the destruction or weakening of the culture of specific milieus – and especially national, regional or professional cultures. In reality there is evidence of a rather different story: the majority of countries or regions have a very specific national culture. Mass culture has taken off particularly where local cultures have declined, for example in major cities. There is no paradox in stating that the expansion of mass culture goes hand in hand with the individualization of cultural practices. Socially defined cultures become less important than inter-personal relationships and the images brought to us by new technologies, the mass nature of which increases the possibil-ity of penetrating to the depths of the collective experience and imagination. Mass culture has greater and greater impact but it is also forming closer links with personal experience, as the use of the internet clearly demonstrates. None of which, of course, prevents this mass culture from dragging in its wake 'products' which are extremely low grade, and which are more and more widely available.

For some considerable time now, the misconception of those who see mass culture as a means of protecting the elite and of destroying the capacity for action of those opposed to authority has been turned on its head by sociologists, begin-ning with Paul Lazarsfeld.

These sociologists have demonstrated the complemen-tarity between, on the one hand, the universalism of the Enlightenment and, on the other, the distinctiveness of all the different ways in which the subject manifests itself in par-ticular situations, whether individual or collective. We need to rid ourselves, once and for all, of the pointless distinction between high culture and popular culture, since we find in the greatest works themes which have been spread through-out the world, thanks to modern methods of dissemination.

# 5

# Profit versus rights

If the crisis itself, along with its causes and consequences, could be explained purely in terms of economic context, we could simply focus our attention on identifying the conditions required in order to emerge from it.

But, as Robert Reich, former Secretary of Labor to President Clinton stressed, this vision is clearly too narrow. For him, the crisis currently affecting us is a systemic rather than a cyclical one.

Sociologists too share the view that we are in the throes of something other than a straightforward economic crisis. And if we are to successfully resist the threat of destruction, we need to identify a principle strong enough to mobilize us against the omnipotence of profit: only a principle which is moral as well as social can stand up to the power of money. Reformers, along with revolutionaries, have known this all along.

### How can we protect ourselves?

We already know that the crisis is a global one, that it destroys all individual interests and imposes on everyone the impersonal law of maximum profit. It is therefore *above and beyond* the social sphere that we need to seek the means to resist a power which itself emanates from the forces that are destroying both social and political life: the globalization of economic activity and the profit motive.

The first to understand this were the *anti-globalists*, but they failed to go beyond economic criticism and did not propose any viable solution.

The more moderate and more realistic groups who call for 'sustainable development' went along with Al Gore in his denunciation of the dangers threatening life on the planet. But they have always confined themselves to mobilizing emotions and ideas, which, according to them, is the only way to mobilize resistance against the forces of destruction. In any case, both sides adopt a stance which is above and beyond the social.

Going beyond the strictly social aspects of the crisis does not imply that any human intervention is considered impossible but, and this is a very different matter, that any fair representation of human beings and their rights can no longer be based on purely social grounds. This is something that religions have always known, driven as they are by a logic which reduces the role of human intervention to a minimum, insofar as this places the principle of the defence of human rights as far removed as possible from social experience. For them, only 'supra-human' forces are capable of 'moving mountains' and resisting the logic of vested interest. We must share with them an image of human beings which is not exclusively a social one and reject the over simplification of positivism.

We have already witnessed clashes between two opposing forces, neither of which could be regarded as social given that one was based on the logic of exploitation and the other on a spirit of resistance. The disappearance of the social dimension, at this highest level, leaves us with the confrontation between an approach based on *calculation* and one based on *conscience*, which refuses to be reduced to material needs and which asserts with growing clarity that the principles, rules and organizational structures of a society must be legitimized by their impact on this self-awareness. Our world is thus dominated by the clash between two principles, *neither of which is social*, but which could respectively be described as 'natural' and 'spiritual', the latter with reference to the fact that it is based on the awareness of human beings that they possess rights and understand their own raison d'être. Does this mean that the individual is an invention of the gods? No. On the contrary, it is the gods that are the inventions of men, as the representation of their basic rights which go beyond any social organization. Anthropomorphic images are of less and less use to us given that the current situation is about the introduction, in an individual or group, of rights which are those of the human subject, and which bring the empirical individual his rights and his conception of Good and Evil. The approaches adopted by religions and by contemporary moral thought are thus parallel and opposed but not contradictory. And if the idea of the subject cannot be regarded as a modern version of the religious spirit, we can at least say that *religions* are 'veiled', externalized, more distanced versions of the subject.

Those areas where the Christian tradition dominates have been quicker than others to grasp the dual nature of every human being, conceived as the image of God made man and of the Man-God. The existence of concepts such as these explains why Christians were the main founders of modern morality. They discovered that within each individual, even though largely dominated by natural needs, was the Subject, which for Christians represented God the creator. This refocusing of the human being on itself, and therefore the elimination of indirect 'veiled' forms of the subject, has enabled the modern world (certain parts of it at least) to become aware of the direct opposition existing between, on the one hand, a logic based on the natural and physical and, on the other, one based on conscience. For the latter enables the human subject to recognize its role as the bearer of its own legitimacy and assures the individual of rights which become universal rights.

The elimination of the social context has not confined us to a world of needs and individual acts of 'pure reality', as Jean Baudrillard critically implies. On the contrary, it has increasingly led us to place the threatened individual under the protection of the individual-subject, creator of his or her own values in the context of both individual and collective behaviour.

Why should we dismiss as unrealistic the idea that the gods transformed themselves into men – men who discover within themselves their dual nature as individuals and as subjects, and who introduce into their individual existence their rights as human subjects? Religions must at all costs be desocialized, separated from the economic and political, ethnic or generic powers they have been associated with. For it is when the social meanings of religions disappear that they are best able to exert their non-social influence. It is then that they can be identified as the 'veiled' forms of the universal rights of human beings.

This universalism, as we are well aware, emerges at the end of many very different paths. And, if there is only *one modernity*, there are *many paths to modernization*. In any case, the contemporary history of morality is largely about the decline of the sacred, with, in its place, man's own creation of himself and each individual's acquisition of universal human rights – rights which represent the categories of Good and Evil.


## The application of morality

Why should we not insist on the use of morality, enriched by the notion of ethics, when moral principles need to be applied to particular situations? The concepts of equality, of justice and of solidarity are after all the bedrock of political and judicial systems, themselves a fundamental part of democratic life, since nothing can be more dangerous, as we know only too well, than to submit judicial decisions to the interests and pride of princes. The practice of the law must, on the contrary, do all it can to improve the situation of the dominated, while still respecting the role of the dominators, provided this does not have a detrimental effect on the rights of all. Over the course of the last half century, we have made considerable progress in this domain. Immediately after the Second World War, the Universal Declaration of Human Rights, initiated under Eleanor Roosevelt and drawn up by the United Nations under the influence of René Cassin, was initially intended as a means of combating the totalitarianism and violence which had escalated following the destruction of all previous controls over behaviour. But as concrete rights were increasingly trampled under foot, we have seen a growing emphasis on the defence of rights of an increasingly ethical nature: the rights of the sick, of prisoners or of national minorities, whether ethnic or religious, the rights of homosexuals and those of other groups who practise forms of sexual relations still deemed illegal. In all these walks of life, moral interests have asserted themselves, which though they have not succeeded in overturning those in power, have provided new mechanisms for the defence of universal rights. It became possible to discuss, or even reject, the right of *intervention* as championed by Mario Bettati and Bernard Kouchner. For all that, this debate introduced the notion that national sovereignty has its limits and that these are breached whenever fundamental rights are infringed within the borders of a nation. There are more and more ethical or moral principles capable of transforming those who fail to respect them into criminals who, in certain particularly serious cases, we must condemn for their role in organizing massacres or even genocides.

The ultimate goal must be, and this cannot be emphasized enough, to separate basic human rights from social ideologies. Temporal power and spiritual power drifted further and further apart in Western Europe and in North America, until the brutal backwards step represented by the emergence of totalitarian regimes. Today we must launch the most vigorous possible attack on those who confuse the law with social authority, by integrating human rights as closely as possible into daily life. Ethics committees and people's tribunals are right in insisting that the recognition by the guilty of their crimes is a necessary pre-condition to them asking their victims for forgiveness. NGOs, groups of pilgrims or of people seeking self-awareness, are growing in importance and in influence, at a time when the major religious institutions continue to decline. Gradually, conscience is placed above the law, and the law above interests and identities. This does not of course mean that morality is gaining the upper hand over power, but more simply that moral judgement is becoming more closely linked to individual behaviour. Thus the most practical decisions are no longer made on the basis of principles and laws. As an illustration of this trend, in the field of clinical medicine, ethical protocols are established at the patient's bedside so that any decisions take the fullest possible account of the views of all concerned, including both the patient and their relatives.

The growing importance of ethically based opinions and behaviour does not, however, transform our society into a Garden of Eden, since the more Good and Evil are acknowledged as criteria for our present actions, the more we sense the hostile opinion surrounding those leaders who find themselves threatened by ethical judgements. We emerge from a twentieth century torn apart by wars, dictatorships and totalitarian regimes and this affirmation of an ethical approach feels almost like the revenge of history, for the invocation of human rights almost inevitably conflicts with the pride of gods and kings. What a long way we have come from the once widely supported notion that wars are merely the result of conflicts of interest in a secularized world! And how could we accept such a superficially optimistic vision at a time when so many parts of the world have been ravaged by wars and mass killings? Those who rejoiced in the demise of the main religions and of all things sacred were quickly proved wrong in the face of historical reality. The almost permanent presence of war, massacres and torture has forced us to associate the modern definition of rights with a conception of individuals no longer as social beings, but as bearers of universal rights. The more the individual is caught up in conflicts, the more the social void and the loss of social norms and values invite us to define the scope of these conflicts in terms which are almost the opposite of the ones with which we have long been satisfied. *Secularization*, in this sense, does not imply the elimination of gods and the sacred; instead it increasingly obliges us to be more and more directly involved in struggles where the 'globalized' forces of interests and of power wage war on human beings who can only count on themselves to assert and ensure respect for their rights. This is not about a return to the past, but a step forward forced upon us by a future which threatens to hold even worse catastrophes than those we have experienced hitherto. It is on the fringes of burning cities that we seek those who see themselves as the bearers of the universal rights of the human subject. This vision should in no way be a daunting one, as though we were too weak to fight against the monsters. The upholders of Good have grown in strength at least as quickly as those responsible for Evil. Even when we feel threatened, each of us is increasingly conscious of the stand we need to make, alone or with others, against the storms unleashed by those in power.

We may perhaps never before in history have seen as many executioners or as many people burned at the stake as in the twentieth century, but it is equally true that this century has also produced at least as many voluntary recruits, heroes and martyrs as any in the past.

## How to mobilize the victims of the crisis?

The major battles of our time are therefore waged either for or against human rights, and no longer in order to impose one or another form of ownership and of power.

Those who thought that globalization and the vast amounts of capital in play would make it impossible for victims to defend themselves against the new masters of the world have been proved wrong. It is true that in a rapidly changing world, any attempt to protect the status quo or national frontiers is doomed to failure. But the same is not true when it comes to the defence of rights or the marshalling of resources in order to place them at the service of human rights, without, however, jeopardizing the survival of businesses or governments by doing so. There is nothing artificial or elitist about such an argument, leading as it does to debates on subjects such as the purpose of education, the relationship between man and machines and management practices, the liberation of women or even town planning and the renewal of democracy.

Conflicts must occupy a central place in any analysis. It is not enough to seek equilibrium between opposing interests and it would be absurd to suggest that salaries and profits should be on a par. Domination, the destruction of assets and of people can only be limited or eliminated through actions on a vast scale, ranging from the evolution of ideas to state interventions.

Some people object to this point of view on the grounds that it is too general and too distant, at a time when the main aim should be to get the financial system back on its feet, and then to kick-start the economy and focus on reinvigorating the job market, which, they are all too aware, will be a long process. But have these people provided us with the formula to prevent future crises and, when they occur, to heal the wounds they inflict?

There can be no doubt that such goals, aimed at protecting the rights of every individual, demand better management, more accurate forecasts and well-managed public aid. But such remedies will never be applied unless they are demanded by a majority of people and strongly supported by mainstream public opinion.

It is clearly not a matter of settling for painless generalities. On the contrary, our aim is to designate forces capable of reducing the role of profit, since this is what destroys cultures and individuals and rejects the poor and the socially excluded, all of whom are accused of hindering the race for maximum profit. The battle for social rights was successful in curtailing the arbitrary behaviour of employers; the battle for cultural rights, though it has not yet achieved its aims, is just as crucial.

During the early stages of a crisis, proposals such as these fall on deaf ears. All we ask of economists and of governments at such times is to halt the crisis and get the economy moving again. But when catastrophe seems less inevitable, everyone's attention turns once again to the future, for the best experts are of the opinion that we would not survive another crisis of the same type. It is therefore time to beat the drum and mobilize all those seeking to combat the threat.

## Ways out of the crisis

Need we be reminded that at the height of the crisis, when the American government decided not to intervene to prevent the collapse of Lehman Brothers, President George W. Bush was in power in the United States, advised in economic matters by Ben Bernanke, President of the FED and successor to Alan Greenspan, as well as by the Treasury Department. Right up to the end, President Bush sought to reassure Americans by minimizing the gravity of the crisis and by expressing the conviction that it would be speedily resolved. American public opinion, and therefore world opinion, was never given any official analysis of the causes of the crisis, which many considered to be the bursting of yet one more 'bubble', following those associated with new technologies and with the subprime mortgage crisis where loans were offered despite insufficient guarantees. The catastrophe, which struck millions of Americans and led to them losing their homes, was not acknowledged by the political powers as a national crisis with the most severe consequences. As Joseph Stiglitz graphically put it, Wall Street was not interested in Main Street, in other words in ordinary Americans. At the same time, Great Britain found itself in similar circumstances and was even more severely affected, despite having a Labour government.

When Barack Obama was elected in January 2009, he found himself facing an extremely dangerous situation: the financial crisis and the banking paralysis were threatening to hold back the productive economy, suffocated by the lack of credit and investment.

Some, like Joseph Stiglitz himself, who had played an important role during Bill Clinton's administration, then accused President Obama of bowing to the interests of the major banks even though these were responsible for the crisis and had no intention of reducing the substantial bonuses they awarded to those at the top. But it was imperative to respond to the emergency and prevent a return of the events of 1929, when unemployment abruptly cast a large proportion of middle- and working-class people into poverty. Moreover, as the major banks and companies who had benefited from aid were quick to discharge their debts out of fear of de facto nationalization, these massive loans generated interest which enabled the government to help the small local banks who were financing SMEs and to support employment.

But it would, however, be wrong to accuse the White House of serving the interests of Wall Street; in fact, the financial crisis, the product of a long series of errors and particularly of an economic mind-set incapable of facing up to reality, meant that the government had little margin for manoeuvre.

Apart from the dissatisfaction symbolized by the Democrats' loss of Massachusetts, the first year of Barack Obama's administration saw an easing of the crisis – though its severity still means that the average American's standard of living has not yet regained the level it had reached at the beginning of the century, the victims of the subprime crisis can still be counted in millions and the renewed 'successes' of the bankers have had a substantial impact on the increased levels of inequality in the country as a whole. The same negative characteristic is also evident in Great Britain. Amongst the Western European countries, Germany is the only exception, to the extent that it has come under criticism from its partner countries for maintaining workers' salaries at a relatively low level in order to stimulate exports, with a consequently negative effect on its competitor-partners. Throughout the continent, numerous countries find themselves crippled under the weight of their debts. The unavoidable rescue of Greece, victim of its own poor management, thus sparked off huge tensions amongst the European countries and, shortly afterwards, the serious nature of the Portuguese crisis further contributed to the weakening of the euro, which dropped to 1.20 against the dollar. Not that this is necessarily bad news for Europe as a whole since it had until then complained about the under-valuation of the dollar (like that of the yuan).

From a global point of view, Europe finds itself increasingly paralysed by the image of its own historic decline, which will inevitably be accelerated by the (very feeble) growth forecast for the entire decade. The new system of government within the European Union further emphasizes this sense of helplessness, which Europeans, particularly those who have already learned to think on a global scale, are painfully aware of. The second part of this book sets out to restore their hopes.

### Reading Joseph Stiglitz

Joseph Stiglitz was one of the few economists to have predicted the major crisis which culminated in 2008, but which he had already detected signs of since the 1970s and the fall of the United States and the world. He describes this in what his French editor called *The Triumph of Greed* (*Le Triomphe de la cupidité*), a title which lacks some of the force of the original, *Freefall*, published by Norton in New York at the beginning of 2010. It is a title full of despair, especially since the second part of the book is an inventory of the principal problems threatening our world: the lack of global demand, the challenges involved in regulating the banking system and in transforming the global economy in order to ensure a fairer allocation of resources. In other words, the fight against poverty, speculation and the domination of the world by money.

In his analysis of the crisis he identifies the actors, and therefore those who are responsible, and condemns, with what may seem excessive severity, Barack Obama and those around him whose task was to turn around the economy and who failed, largely because they were unable to free themselves (almost to the same extent, he argues, as those responsible for the crisis) from the domination of those financiers whose serious errors mobilized all the state's resources and who were all too quick to resume their deadly game. But when it comes to considering how to trace a path from Evil back to Good, this is outside the actors' sphere of interest and the economist seems to concentrate solely on telling the truth – an admirable goal, of course, but one which leaves the initial question unanswered: where did the Evil come from? Why did the United States plunge into a policy of lies and of irresponsibility, exhausting their savings and accumulating debts, not only for the government but also for millions of families?

It is necessary, though by no means enough, to call into question the maestro, Alan Greenspan, and his pupil, Ben Bernanke. Why did Congress, intellectuals, the media and the unions fail to raise the alarm? The reason for this silence and these mistakes lies in the fact that high principles and sound ideas are no match for actions which flatter the population, happy to live beyond their means and full of pride at the idea that they dominate the world, while in reality they have long been paving the way for the bursting of the latest bubble, the subprime crisis, which is about to explode. The economist, renowned as he is for his knowledge and for his burning sense of justice and deep concern for the poorest people, seems inexorably driven to do the very thing with which sociologists are often reproached: meeting force with ideas, strategies with principles, interests with ideals.

Hence the effort made here, despite the inherent difficulties of the task, to define the actors and the categories of action most likely to contribute to finding a way out of the crisis; one which, however clearly defined, cannot be reduced to a simple conflict between Good and Evil.

Such questions can be justified because the person they set out to challenge is J. Stiglitz, a very great economist, and undoubtedly one of the most perceptive. When we examine the work of economists who lack the same depth and are less well known, we cannot fail to notice their silence on the issue of how to find a way out of the crisis.

Essentially my sense of dissatisfaction on reading Stiglitz stems largely from the absence of actors in his analysis. Yet, the only possible response to the questions I have just raised must involve a radical shaking up of ideas, in full awareness that the creation of an economy and a society is never entirely governed by the facts themselves, given that these are no more stable than a mirage.

We should no longer expect the economy to form the building blocks of society. We cannot even settle any longer for the idea of 'limited rationality', which generated countless analyses ranging from Michel Crozier to Herbert Simon. Moreover, Joseph Stiglitz demonstrates the ineffectiveness of compromises and half-measures. It is perhaps this which makes his work one of the finest contributions to a new approach to actors. But his ambition stops there.

This is why, for my part, I have placed at the centre of the analysis the idea that, in situations dominated by globalization, the only principle on which a social organization can be constructed is not the individual and his needs but the *subject* and its rights – the rights of human beings to be recognized as the arbiters of their own choices, in other words to be recognized as subjects possessing rights. Only the subject who is aware of his rights can stand up to the all-powerful force of globalization and to neoliberalism, which has subjugated both the economy and human beings to the market, this latter being deemed more rational than the decisions emanating from people and from institutions.

But this notion of subject involves more than simply the defence of human rights. It is made up of all that is recognized as universal in the human being, beginning with reason, which defines the truth outside of religious or political ideologies, experience or tradition. Yet truth is predominantly brought to us by science, a domain in which the findings are constantly enriched by the work of other scientists.

This is why the technical and scientific creation of new techniques and products should be at the heart of a policy centred on the subject. At a time when many people see the globalization of markets to be the defining principle of the economy, it is worth remembering that innovation has brought the economy more resources than has the accumulation of capital. And far from reducing the United States to being merely the stage for a neoliberalism without actors, it is important to remember that this country is also, far more than any other, the greatest inventor and the greatest creator of techniques and of products. Many criticisms have been made of the Schumpeterian notion of the entrepreneur, yet it does at least accord a central place to invention and creation within economic analysis.

Modes of analysis and of evaluation in these fields are developing as much in open opposition to the effects of globalization as in the quest for a compromise between human rights and economic creation. Any attempt to construct a society without any reference to its economic activities would be tantamount to falling from Scylla into Charybdis, given that these are precisely the instruments needed for the creation of a new social world. Economic life and social life can only be saved together and insofar as the actors want it to happen.

We must not forget that any recourse to higher principles capable of resisting the internal logic of globalization and the hegemony of financial capital only makes sense if these principles are transformed into norms and modes of organization in all aspects of society, as much in work and production as in school and the family. And when it comes to legal matters, the defence of freedom and of rights must always take precedence over the defence of property and the organization of trade. None of this is new, since in all societal types, the central principle, whether it be God, the Church, the Prince or Progress, is present in all aspects of social life and sets the direction. But it is to this reinvention of an ethical principle, expression of the moral in specific social situations, that the social sciences must give priority.

After this admiring if critical reading of Stiglitz, we are better equipped to envisage what form a new societal type, capable of saving us from catastrophe, might take.

# Part Two

## A possible society

# 6

# The hypothesis

The long-term evolution of a society and that of an economic crisis seem at first sight to have little in common, since the causes of the current crisis, like those of so many others, were financial ones resulting from excess liquidity, the availability of credits far in excess of the actual value of the assets on which they were secured, and the massive, uncontrolled development of derivatives. Against this background of a relentless quest for profit, the subprime crisis, followed by the collapse of a major New York bank, had catastrophic consequences on the economy at large.

The economic crisis effectively acts as a barrier to the formation of a new society, of new economic actors and of the relationships between them. From this point of view, the crisis cannot be defined as just a breakdown of capitalist society. We need to begin by acknowledging that it destroys society wherever it erupts.

A major economic and financial crisis, like that of 1929 or the one we are currently experiencing, obliterates the actors, their conflicts and all forms of mediation and of arbitration. Those who control the financial system exclusively in their own interests, who oppose those both of companies, particularly small- or medium-sized ones, and of the workforce, become so far removed from society and its institutions that they often end up acting illegally by creating a huge private equity sector completely outside any public control.

These financiers effectively step outside the framework of capitalist society and enter an illegal world in the same way as do drug cartels, arms dealers or cigarette smugglers. Their actions are part of the powerful surge in an expanding illegal economy. All of which bears no resemblance to capitalist society as it has just been defined. The most important social repercussion of these barbaric actions is the significant and enduring increase in unemployment, a delayed effect of the financial crisis. But the hypothesis that this crisis may yet take a more positive turn cannot be entirely rejected.

### Three erroneous hypotheses

Four possible hypotheses can be envisaged. The *first* involves a return to the pre-existing status quo, in other words, to *business as usual*. The *second* involves an enduring weakening of all social actors, and even of the state, in a situation dominated by economic upheaval. These two hypotheses must be ruled out, given the scale both of the enormous losses suffered and of the level of state interventions. On the other hand, economists and commentators are often in agreement about the end of American hegemony, partly as a result of America's risky military intervention against Muslim countries, but more importantly because the American economy is largely controlled by the very people who encouraged over-indebtedness and speculation with no concern for improving the real economy.

The *third* hypothesis could be called the Tocqueville hypothesis, insofar as in studying the economic causes of the French Revolution, as set out in *The Old Regime and the Revolution*, Tocqueville found that the reign of Louis XVI was the most prosperous period in the entire monarchy. It is precisely this improvement in conditions, in comparison with the first half of the eighteenth century, a period marked by pessimism and by the lack of any prospects, that Tocqueville identifies as one of the principle explanations of the Revolution. The generalized recovery, brought about thanks to Turgot and Necker, gave French people a renewed sense that they could forge their own future. Today this hypothesis can be reformulated in the following manner: when the Western economies start to recover, and when some of the major emerging economies begin to overcome their weaknesses, might we not here and there see the emergence of powerful protest movements but also of more positive proposals for the construction of a new type of society? Can we avoid a violent swing of the pendulum in places where, as in the United States, social inequality has increased and even, in the period 2000–8, rocketed, due largely to the dramatic rise in the level of the very highest incomes? Even in those countries where trade unions offer little support for protests, might we not expect a similar explosion to those which hit France in 1936 and 1947? There is nothing which would *a priori* exclude that possibility, particularly since even at the most violent moment of the crisis no large-scale mobilization occurred. A few centres of resistance did form, created by certain groups of workers protesting against the closure or relocation of a business, but this was largely before the crisis had become generalized. This kind of mobilization could possibly occur in a particular country in the context of a presidential campaign. But even if this were to happen, any associated movements would be more about social unrest than economic pressure and would be unlikely to contribute to the re-establishment of a system of actors. After so many years during which trade unions and collective bargaining became steadily weaker, it is unlikely that we will see any re-building of the social relationships which were characteristic of industrial (and post-industrial) societies. In the same way, the liberation of businesses from the domination of financial capital is far from guaranteed; any return to the era where John K. Galbraith vaunted the victory of the executives is extremely unlikely.

All three hypotheses succeed in conjuring up complex and evolving situations, yet none of them believes in the reconstruction of the industrial society with its focus on manufacturing underpinned by new technologies and the central role it gives to major companies and to new-style unions as well as to new methods of collective bargaining.

### From the third to the fourth hypothesis

It would be unfair, and even irresponsible, to conclude *a priori* that regulation of financial dealings is impossible, even if it is true that such dealings, within the global financial system, have far outstripped those transacted between the financial system and the economic system. In his most recent book, *Penser la crise* (Fayard, 2010), Élie Cohen looks in detail at the suggestions usually put forward as a way out of the crisis and the solutions most frequently advanced.

Many suggestions have been made to improve the way credit ratings agencies work, and, on a more general level, other proposals have been put forward, in particular by certain senior British figures (and notably Adair Turner, director of the Financial Services Authority), with a view to the introduction of a sort of Tobin tax levied on transactions. German and French governments rallied to this proposal in 2012. Mervyn King, in his role as governor of the Bank of England, subsequently echoed by other experts, suggested a separation of the various banking functions, in particular those of retail and investment banking. Others suggest dismantling the current system in a more rigorous way, by separating four types of operations: retail banking, investment banking, asset management and insurance (Cohen, 2010, p. 335) – a suggestion that nevertheless comes up against the objection that the banks offering a full range of services were the ones which coped best during the crisis.

Be that as it may, even if progress has been made, if the FED (but also the Central European Bank) have played a positive role, and if the American government, with the support of certain European governments, prevented a systemic crisis from erupting after the fall of Lehman Brothers, it is still difficult to believe that we currently have access to the regulatory tools needed by every country, beginning with the United States, and by the global economy as a whole.

Which brings us back once again to the biggest problem facing the global economy, one which is far more significant than the exorbitant bonuses paid to traders and hedge fund managers.

We need to remember that the most serious problem facing the world economy is the absence of savings and the enormous debts of the United States, which favour the predominantly export-led policy of China, Germany and, in spite of its long period of crisis, Japan. A policy which may well seem shocking because it stands in the way of any improvement in the living standards of a huge number of people. But is it not mere tautology to criticize major economic policies, of which the poor are the main victims, and to try to put an end to the excessive power of the financial economy, given that this was largely the result of excessive liquidity and a quest for pure profit divorced from any positive economic effect?

While recognizing the value of financial analyses, or even more broadly economic ones, it is clear that we need to go further.

A crisis as serious as the one we are experiencing cannot be dealt with without an analysis of the economic transformations responsible for creating imbalances which end up making some people more vulnerable while others get richer. Can this crisis, dating back as it does to the end of the twentieth century, be fully understood unless account is taken of the transformation that has occurred in terms of economic activity? While the Bretton Woods system was in operation, in other words, for the duration of the period of recovery experienced by the global economy in the wake of the violent shocks provoked by world war and totalitarian regimes, world industry was given a new boost, thanks to five-year plans, the spread of new production methods of the type introduced by Ford, and automation. Following this, rapid technological developments, and in particular the expansion of world trade, created new areas which the financial system put to its own use for non-economic purposes. Could the same have happened in a society still dominated by major industrial enterprises? It came as a shock to see General Motors and Chrysler depending on the government for their survival, just like Citibank, rescued from bankruptcy on a number of occasions.

It is difficult to qualify our current situation in terms of its levels of activity. With the exception of Germany, which still shares with China the top position in terms of global industrial exports, industry is declining in importance in the more developed countries. And yet we know that the expression 'post-industrial society' is misleading.

The best way of describing the current situation is in fact to say that it represents the total separation between an increasingly globalized economic world and a society which is itself largely destroyed by this separation, since the internal organization of a society is normally linked to its 'external' activity, in other words to its labour, production and economic activity as a whole. Faced with the imposing (and at the same time threatening) scale of the globalized economy, the world of social institutions no longer has any internal coherence or function. Instead, it has become a universe of doubt and confusion where normal rules no longer apply. The significance of the present moment is that this split between the economic world and the social world is both normal and pathological. Normal, in that it marks the end of a profound transformation of those economies within which economy, society and politics were intimately linked. Pathological, because the crisis shatters the elements which were already in the process of separating from each other and acts as a barrier to the creation of new forms of social organization. The crisis cannot, of course, bring an end to the transformation of economic life, but it represents a major obstacle to any attempts at reconstructing the social fabric, even when such efforts originate outside society, as is (also) the case with regard to the globalized economy.

This *dual meaning* – normal and pathological – of the split between the economy and society constitutes the necessary starting point for any analysis of the aftermath of the crisis and of the possible futures it will lead to.

These analyses, significant as they may be, offer no solution to the immediate problems threatening us. They should nevertheless incite us to look further ahead and to renew the action we took at the end of the post-war period of industrial recovery, in other words to identify a new societal type, in its broadest sense.

## The fourth hypothesis

In fact, we find ourselves confronted with two possible futures, both of which represent a break with the past. One is a hopeless one; the other brings new hope. By definition, neither of them is certain. It is as easy to fall back again as it is to move forwards.

### (a) *The dark future*

At the beginning of 2010, the combination of a recovery in the banking sector, a slight improvement in international trade, and even, in certain countries, the beginnings of a return to growth – albeit very limited and (except in Canada) without any impact on unemployment levels – led some people to think that the Western world of Europe and North America was indeed capable of emerging from the crisis. This optimism was largely unfounded, since at that very moment a second crisis was already looming. In 2009, as we have already pointed out, governments everywhere had intervened to limit the crisis, which had reached its peak in 2008. This proved useful but produced two consequences which were to become more and more difficult to live with. The first of these was the increase in the budgetary deficits of these countries, which led to them ignoring commitments previously undertaken, in accordance with the European Budgetary Pact, limiting the deficit to less than 3 per cent of GNP. In both the United Kingdom and Greece the deficit reached 11 per cent and in France it reached 8 per cent in 2010. The second consequence was the increase in public debt, which in certain countries ended up amounting to more than 100 per cent of GDP.

Faced with these threats, governments could scarcely increase state spending by raising taxes since this would have produced a third crisis of growth. The measures currently being adopted in France, such as the non-replacement of half of all civil servants reaching retirement age, are provoking violent protests, particularly amongst teachers and health workers. Germany alone remains stable, but only because it has chosen to limit real salaries in order to expand exports, often at the expense of its neighbours, and in particular of France, which after a long period of substantial surpluses has sunk into a deep trade deficit.

This serious and unstable situation has seen the eruption of a new crisis in Greece and the emergence of serious threats against a number of other countries.

The situation of Greece was an unusual one. The figures it had provided to Brussels had been massaged in a way that seriously underestimated the extent of the country's failure; corruption was rife and, as in many other European countries, income from tourism, crucial to its stability, had been dwindling since 2007. Ratings agencies made the crisis worse by lowering the rating not only of Greece, but also of Portugal and Spain, forcing these countries to borrow at ever higher rates. Greece was on the brink of the abyss, to the extent that some even suggested it should leave the Eurozone and indeed the European Union – a solution which would probably have proved fatal to the entire European system.

European Union and IMF aid to Greece was slow to materialize, owing to the resistance of Germany and to Chancellor Angela Merkel's (justified) fears of losing an important regional election as a result of such support. As a result, the situation in Greece continued to deteriorate. In the end, Greece needed only 110 billion euros and these were made available. In Portugal, where the main exports and tourism had been badly hit, the situation similarly deteriorated in this climate of panic induced by the sight of a state reduced to bankruptcy, a hypothesis which had not been envisaged in any European treaties ...

In Spain, the economy was affected right from the beginning of the American subprime crisis because, in order to compensate for de-industrialization, Spain had placed its hopes for the future in tourism, in other words in the construction industry. Even Barcelona, once so heavily industrialized, had seen the decline of its traditional industries, particularly textiles, and found itself relying on tourism for survival. The construction sector, after a period of rapid expansion, duly collapsed and saw its activity reduced by two-thirds in the space of just a few months. Public opinion was unleashed against the hitherto extremely popular president of the Council of Ministers, the socialist Zapatero. The Spanish banking system with its network of *cajas* (savings banks) has been severely weakened as a result of the property crisis. The fall of Spain would entail the collapse of the entire Eurozone and in fact of the whole European project.

Fortunately, the Eurozone countries took drastic measures in order to protect the threatened economies. Yet it is by no means certain that plans to reduce the deficit in public finances will not provoke violent reactions in some countries, as was the case in Greece where the Communist Party was responsible for a growing number of violent incidents, culminating in the death of three people in a bank.

Without sinking into pessimism, we need to recognize that what we are witnessing may indeed herald the decline of Europe. The helplessness of the European Union is watched on all sides with anxiety and disappointment. The EU failed to take any significant measure to regulate financial operations. The resistance of the City in Great Britain was undoubtedly a factor in this failure to act, but still does not justify it. As for European leaders, there is ample evidence that they do not view the weakness of Brussels in an altogether unfavourable light.

South America has proved more resistant to the crisis than Europe. The state-owned banks, led by the Brazilian BNDE, have introduced excellent countercyclical policies. Chile and Peru have amassed significant budgetary surpluses, enabling them to face the crisis. Brazil, whose worldwide importance is recognized, has now supplanted a Mercosur destroyed by the widening gap between Brazil and Argentina. As for Chile, it is, with the exception of China, the developing country which has made the most significant progress.

The same cannot be said, it is true, of Central America, the Caribbean and Mexico, all completely dependent on the United States and, in the case of Mexico, devastated by the ravages of drug trafficking. As a result, South America now has closer relations with Asia, and in particular with China, than with the United States and Europe.

Anyone seeking to assess the situation in which Europe now finds itself would certainly be making a grave error if they failed to recognize the key significance of the decline in the international position of our continent, a threat too long masked by the illusions spread by those pro-Europeans anxious above all to integrate the continent into a world economy globalized and dominated by the United States – and more particularly by the financiers themselves. It is true that the gravity of the situation was finally grasped by European leaders, particularly those of France and Germany, inciting them in May 2010 to set up a relief fund for countries in difficulty, which was increased a month later.

This important decision could well prevent a new catastrophe, but nothing will stand in the way of the speculator's quest for profit at any price. These speculators will continue to destabilize the weakest economies abetted by the ratings agencies. The euro is not out of danger. The hypothesis of a new crisis cannot be excluded and, were this to occur, it could lead to a catastrophic series of crises.

## (b) *The open future*

This second part of the fourth hypothesis is more difficult to formulate. The absence of any widespread social and political reactions during this crisis, the most striking feature of which was the triumph of financial capital over the real economy, took everyone by surprise. The crisis did not lead to the strengthening of either the left or of the unions. A social conflict is a clash between opposing social groups battling over a share of the results of growth, with both sides mutually acknowledging the positive value of the issues being contested. A social conflict is consequently very different from an economic crisis. The intervention of the major industrial states enabled the banks to recover, without however introducing any significant changes to the economic system, in spite of the fact that the banks' activities and methods are more strictly controlled than in the past. At the end of 2009, if President Obama did indeed rescue the Western economy, it was nevertheless not within his power to restructure the system of socio-economic relationships and conflicts which had characterized the industrial society. Up to now there has been no sign of any significant conflict between clearly defined actors; there is no evidence of any issues shared by two opposing sides: the new society has not yet taken shape. But there are signs that it is imminent and this is what the fourth hypothesis is about. This hypothesis is a difficult one to set out because it involves the construction of a new system of actors as yet impossible to describe. Needless to say, this transition to a new society implies the transformation of our existing institutions, which, in everyday terms, we refer to as the crises of our cities, of democracy, of justice, of education or of the family. This separation of the economic world from society characterizes the current situation, particularly because globalization elevates the economy to a level which places it beyond the intervention of any social, political or even economic institution. Hence the phenomenon we have already drawn attention to: the absence of any organized reactions by workers and by the population in general. It is important at this stage in the argument to acknowledge the extreme dissymmetry between an economic world overwhelmed by the financial sphere and any possible scope for social action.

Right from the beginning of his presidency, Barack Obama managed to implement a powerful intervention mechanism which succeeded in preventing the crisis from spreading, but the banks were anxious to redeem their debts as quickly as possible, and the president of the United States had not envisaged nationalizing loss-making banks. This explains the social and political silence around a crisis of such extreme gravity.

In the absence of any social and political project capable of defining new forms of equilibrium, the only spontaneous response to the triumph of the globalized economy will be a defensive communitarianism, which will no longer be defined in terms of social relationships but as a retreat into a religious, national or ethnic identity. This communitarianism could take the (limited) form of economic protectionism, but we must not forget that the confrontations between religious groups and certain centres of the globalized economy have already led to war – jihad against jihad – between radical Islamism and the American and British troops who invaded Iraq, or between Palestinians and the Israeli government, which is currently in the hands of nationalists opposed to any form of negotiation. Such military conflicts have almost nothing in common with any internal struggle for influence between opposing social groups. We need therefore to be on the look-out for any signs indicating the imminent emergence of a force capable of successfully taking on global economic and financial power.

Once again it is the United States that has seen the formation of most women's groups, ecological movements or groups combating racism and supporting civil rights. These have even broadly replaced the vertical intervention of the government by practising an efficient form of *self-government* which, unlike communitarianism, facilitates the formation of local groups focusing on general problems.

But these local associations are often dominated by influential groups which are hostile towards minorities. The impact of this (predominantly Protestant) fundamentalism is enhanced in the United States by the activities of impassioned preachers who encourage isolationism and a rejection of the foreign. There is no religious equivalent of this in Western Europe.

Whether their influence is 'positive' or 'negative', in the United States these core groups collectively limit the power of the state and give civil society a diversity, a flexibility and, above all, a vigour which counterbalances the centralized nature of the political system. But only the assertion of universal values will successfully ensure that the most powerful interests are kept in check.

### Three stages in the birth of the subject: creation, communication, establishment of values

Let us start by avoiding confusion. The birth of the subject has no link to the existence of a post-industrial society based on *communication*. In manufacturing societies, there is a connection between the structural conditions and the choice of values which govern action. Communication is still an element in manufacturing societies but it constitutes the *foundations* of the post-industrial society.

Thus the path is mapped out which leads, via communication networks, from science and economic organization to social actors. What matters here is to recognize the specificity of each stage of the analysis. But above all it is important to emphasize the distance which separates the reference to the subject, as I have formulated it, from problems of communication. The latter, which have constituted the foundations of post-industrial society, have merged the communicators with the content of the message itself. Unlike industrial and post-industrial societies, where the social relations of production and social policies were inseparable, the society currently taking shape can be envisaged as one characterized by the opposition of two non-social principles, on the one hand globalization, and on the other the subject endowed with rights. Between these two mountains stretches a plain where there is intense activity, a network of roads and a concentration of towns and their inhabitants. But the life-giving water supply comes from the mountains.

There can be no life without irrigation, but irrigation depends on a supply of water flowing down from the mountains. If this metaphor is not clear enough, let us reiterate that action takes its purpose *outside the social realm*, both in the economic universe constructed and discovered by men, and in the introspective world of the subject. Is there any clearer way of emphasizing the contrast between the classical vision and the one I am introducing here, which has more affinity with the study of ancient forms of the subject, religious or philosophical, than with a rationalism drawing on the philosophy of history?

## The coming together of two meta-social principles

This notion of the subject, unlike social matters, develops outside the social sphere, under the influence of collective movements which are more cultural than social and which are not motivated by the defence of specific interests. These movements most often develop at the grass roots of society, and challenge decisions imposed by those in power. In countries most committed to the construction of a new society, and in particular in the United States, conflicts between the two sides are so visible that they have become a very important element in electoral choice. Until now, however, the wishes of the government have prevailed. So, for example, the United States refused the Kyoto agreements even though Americans were running huge campaigns against greenhouse gases. We can see the role of the unspoken in the politics of this country as well as in others. Western European countries for their part tend to focus on two main areas: the fight against the economy and its 'global' powers, and the desire to protect their independence, particularly in the cultural domain.

What is important is to have a good understanding of how the two opposing cultural tendencies are diffused throughout society and exercise a powerful influence over political decisions. The extremely rapid growth of new methods of communication – from the mobile phone to the internet, from television channels to magazines dedicated to stars and celebrities – have meant that ideas relating to political ecology and those of anti-racist movements or of groups set up in defence of various minorities, can be spread rapidly, even though they lose some of the force attached to movements more directly linked to the defence of the subject, of its freedom and of equality and justice.

Their main strength lies in the fact that the dangers targeted by current cultural groups are those identified by scientists working outside government control. Many people believed that society and mass culture would destroy politics and in particular social and cultural movements, by drowning them in a universe of advertising where they would simply become invisible. Not very long ago we could still hear those who were claiming that the media world was merely a new version of the *bread and circuses* of the Roman emperors. Such anxiety is indeed partly justified, for many aspects of collective life have been so tarnished by the language of advertising that they have become unintelligible. But the era of an all-powerful media is coming to an end. More and more voices are making themselves heard. The transition from the movements associated with the industrial society to new social and cultural movements has happened very rapidly, and today we would need to block our ears to avoid hearing the ecologists, feminists and those defending nations threatened or already destroyed by genocide.

What has been missing until now is an overview of the new society which is taking shape. We are still deafened by the groups formed to defend 'victims' who spread the notion that it is in fact impossible to combat mass civilization. Let us look instead at the example of Italy, where the VIOLA movement, operating solely through the internet, is targeting the impunity of Silvio Berlusconi.

It is never too early to make a systematic inventory of the changes affecting industrial and post-industrial societies, and to see that the economic crisis affects all aspects of social life. But we have effectively already entered this new universe to which we are constantly referring, and we need at this point to put forward our representations.

We understand better now the need to make a distinction between the financial crisis, which rapidly spread to the economy and to the labour market, and the long-term transformations within society as it moves from industrial or post-industrial production to a situation I have already described as post-social. This point of view has nothing in common with Francis Fukuyama's notion of the end of history; indeed it seeks to challenge that view. We need to reject the idea that all aspects of life within a society are determined by the economic situation, an idea which no longer corresponds to reality. Today the social fabric is dominated on the one hand by the globalized economy, which exerts pressure on all areas of social life, and on the other by the reference of actors to a subject itself defined as existing beyond the social order, belonging instead to the domain of universal principles. The conflict between these two points of view, both of them *beyond* society, spreads until it forms a contradiction, a conflict which can only be resolved through war. Yet this danger will diminish insofar as these two meta-social principles will be embodied in the rules and the modes of decision making which will ensure the logic of each of them becomes part of the social fabric.

Rising inequality calls for changes to be made in terms of the economic organization if we wish to avoid a social conflagration, which would be the last straw for a society already damaged by the crisis. Indeed, the vast majority of people would like to see the government intervene in order to reduce these inequalities. This immediate reaction implies that after the extreme domination of the economy over all other aspects of society, it is time to re-establish links between the economic and non-economic elements of the economic situation: the state of public opinion and the wishes of the government are just as significant as the movements of capital they seek to control.

In the new post-social context, demands go beyond economic objectives; their focus is the defence of the subject, in other words, the rights of all, for the most significant tendency of the changes taking place is to separate the economy from society or culture, without destroying all the links between them. We see too that the economic order and the world of ideas are in opposition to each other, yet still remain linked. Today, conflicts can more easily veer towards an armed struggle than towards limited reformism. What protects us from the catastrophic hypothesis of two worlds implacably opposed to each other is the fact that there is currently space enough to accommodate both these opposing principles. And it is equally impossible to imagine a society focused entirely on the defence of human rights as it is one reduced simply to banking transactions or the manipulation of workers on all levels through the use of management and motivational methods.

In the past, many actors hoped to see capitalism destroyed as a result of pressure from the workforce. Today, the principle danger is, on the contrary, the definitive victory by either the very rich, or the very poor who, lacking any means of influence over society, can easily become disturbing symbols, fascist or prophetic, of the populist ideal. The best way of avoiding such extreme threats is to develop a stronger awareness of the very high stakes associated with conflicts. Today, for example, the demands of the ecologists in fact increase the power of the state to intervene. As for the extreme concentration of wealth, which effectively leaves a great number of workers trapped in poverty and exclusion, this is depicted in such tragic tones that nobody could wish for a return to Victorian capitalism.

It should not be supposed that the enduring power of the subject implies that philosophers, sociologists or writers are the driving force of social unrest. It would be no truer than suggesting that they were responsible for the development of the workers' movement in the nineteenth century whereas in fact they merely wrote the speeches. I have demonstrated elsewhere that the workers' movement should not be reduced to the level of its political outpourings. And Marx himself did more in terms of criticizing capitalism than in understanding the strikes, acts of sabotage and other forms of pressure which workers used against the system; workers who were not acting in ignorance.

Today, awareness of a potential catastrophe is stronger than ever, and environmental politics would lose much of its power if it did not draw on the most deep-rooted rejection of death. The Aztecs did not realize that the Spaniards they welcomed so warmly would end up massacring them. Today, on the contrary, we are sufficiently well informed to be able to predict the catastrophic results of the financiers' triumph. Of course, an awareness of risks is not enough, but it does at least exist, which explains why the environmental movement does not only represent the concerns of a handful of scientists. In any event, we must eliminate any suggestion that either spontaneism or scientific rationalism lies behind the cultural movements already dominating the political scene. What we lack is a sufficiently comprehensive description of the means and effects of the domination of financial capitalism. Over the course of the last two centuries, this has already produced numerous serious crises which have affected every aspect of economic life. But these have become more serious from one period to the next. The 1929 crisis tore the world apart by pushing the Germans into Nazism. The current crisis could lead to a gradual decline in the importance of the Western world and of Europe in particular. Yet at the same time, we are increasingly aware of all the social forces, the cultural practices and the political decisions which make possible, and constantly reinforce, the domination of profit without any compensating economic advantage. Death stalks us ever closer since we saw Hiroshima reduced to dust by an atomic bomb devised by the most eminent scientists.

Today, the rationale of the pursuit of maximum profit and that of respect for the subject and its rights are in conflict with each other. Each of these two principles could be embodied in all sectors of society, but equally they could permeate public interventions, particularly those of the state, which seek to bridge the gap between conflicting principles and to transform contradictions into complementarities.

A crisis, however serious it is, does not determine any given future, even if it effectively shatters links with the past. In the present case, it may indeed result in the breakdown of social and even economic life, bringing with it violence, illegality and ultimately decline. But the destruction of the old links between the economy and society could, in the face of a globalized economy, also favour the formation of groups defending not only economic interests but also individual rights.

## Between two futures

If the crisis alone fails to impose one or the other of these two solutions, the way it is dealt with will have decisive effects on the future. And it is only if the crisis is perceived as a problem to be resolved, and therefore if it contributes to the emergence of new objectives and new forms of choice, that it will be able to contribute to the formation of a new society. On the contrary, the more the crisis is viewed as a situation beyond remedy, as a major geopolitical change, as a consequence of the weakness of economic and political actors, the more likely it is that it will, like an avalanche, sweep away everything in its path.

The extreme contradiction between the accelerated rate of decay of an economic and social system and the creation of a new societal type does preclude the existence of very strong links between the two processes. Many economists have thus stressed the profound changes in economic context and policies caused by the collapse of a type of capitalism, although they almost always cited the role of external factors as an explanation of this turnaround. Roosevelt's New Deal could not have come into being without the 1929 crisis, but it did not revive the American economy – and it was only the war, from 1941 onwards, that enabled full employment to be restored, under the government's guidance.

After the Second World War, in the major countries of non-communist Europe, as well as in many others, 'developmentalist' regimes were formed in which state intervention was all the stronger since the capitalist circles had often disappeared, as a result of their cooperation with the conquering Nazis and subsequent national shame – and often their businesses were even nationalized. This was particularly the case in France, but also in Italy, Great Britain, and even in Germany, where trade union pressure was powerful. New state companies appeared, such as Mattei in Italy and in France a group of very high-ranking civil servants (Massé, Delouvrier, Bloch-Lainé, Gruson, Hirsch, etc.) also played a remarkable role during this period.

The demise of this managed economy in the late 1960s led to the rapid world-wide spread of neoliberal capitalism, a system in which the intervention of non-capitalist elements (whether unions or governments) continued to decline while the number of crises, either by sector or by region, rose.

Three years after the crisis erupted in 2007, very few people believed 'reforms' would be enough to re-establish the system that had previously existed. Similarly to the aftermath of 1929, a profound transformation of economic life seems inevitable. But how can new government intervention pave the way for the new societal model, for what I have referred to as the post-social situation?

The increasingly global nature of the world economy and the extreme autonomy of financial activity, now divorced from the real workings of the economy and from businesses, have inspired numerous attempts to activate changes which can be evaluated in terms of motivation and non-economic processes. The priority must be to fight against the destructive effects of the current economy, in other words to take action in ways that will favour our survival. But it seems equally important to take steps to increase world demand and to reduce the inequalities which have multiplied so rapidly during the course of the last few years.

But any such attempt will be more difficult to achieve than in the past insofar as there is a deeper rift between financial capitalism, chiefly responsible for the latest crisis, and calls to protect the natural balance and to defend human rights. The current political silence cannot last and it is likely that the (difficult) transition towards a new type of society will happen in the heat of the moment rather than after cool consideration.

### From actors to subjects

Initially sociology set out to study systems, functions and the exercise of power. But, particularly since the start of the major social movements of the 1960s, it has moved away from the idea of a 'reciprocity of perspectives' between the system and the actors.

Social psychologists first rediscovered the autonomy of the actor acting within a group, by demonstrating the effects the character of the group had on individual behaviours. Some, in particular Serge Moscovici, went still further and explored the relationship between actors and the culture within which they were operating.

My approach here is not far removed from that of social psychologists but it has less in common with earlier work on 'basic personality'. It aims primarily to identify the links between social reality, whether that of systems or of actors, and the fundamentally different level where moral behaviours are established and find legitimacy. Such behaviours were for a long time primarily of a religious nature, either in the literal sense of the term, or through a belief in secular ideals such as progress or the nation. But at a time when many speak of *secularization*, or in other words the diminishing role of the religious in social behaviours, whether utilitarian or humanitarian, I champion the idea that the religious has become an integral part of mankind, metamorphosing into *humanism*, a pivotal point in the experience of modern-day man.

The more our capacity to act on ourselves and on our environment expands, the more this humanism is strengthened. For a long time it sought to strike a balance between facts and values, and often managed to do so by having recourse to an evolutionist approach. Today, as the globalization of the economy threatens to invade and dominate everything, the time has come to abandon this balancing act. Only the most direct appeal to what must be called the *subject*, as in the Enlightenment, will enable us to combat this invasion. We increasingly make moral, and even spiritual, judgements on our situation and our behaviour. The fact that this tendency is becoming widespread should give us confidence in our future.

# 7

# The post-social situation

## Industrial and post-industrial societies

Let us step back in time in order to gain a better understanding of all the changes currently taking place, or those which have already taken place, in this new society and examine it in the context of those which preceded it, in order to evaluate these changes more clearly.

For a long time, our attention was largely focused on the transition from what was known as the industrial society to what some have referred to as the post-industrial society. Daniel Bell and I were the first to emphasize this transformation. But, as I have already pointed out, these are in fact two separate stages within industrial society. In the same way, since Georges Friedmann, we have taken to distinguishing between a number of different industrial revolutions: a society dominated by coal, a society which harnessed electricity in the service of manufacturing, and finally one which witnessed the birth of the electronic era and, in particular, the development of highly complex communication systems. The differences between these phases of industrial society, significant as they are, did not cause us to shift from one type of society to another. And, as we distance ourselves from these successive transformations, we are better placed to understand what these various stages have in common.

Industrial society can be defined as one where the development of manufacturing and improvements in productivity bring about profound changes, in particular in terms of the social implications of manufacturing. From this perspective, the transition from industrial society to post-industrial society marks a significant new stage but does not represent the transition from one society to another.

In post-industrial society, there is as yet no distinction between the material and the moral world. Indeed, many people have emphasized the links between the two in this type of society where communication introduces a new relationship between the information conveyed and the frame of mind of the communicator. Manuel Castells was the first to recognize the central place of communication in post-industrial societies. His intention was always to show that good communication involves a recognition of the importance of emotions, feelings and ideas in the transmission of messages which, if genuine communication is to take place, must undergo transformation in the process of transferring from sender to receiver. Like Antonio Damasio, author of major studies on the brain, he is critical of all forms of inward-looking rationalism.

But let us not confuse matters. The subject of communication has little in common with the notion of the separation between actors and system. It is in the post-industrial society that communication occupies a central place, not in the post-social situation.

For all that, it is from the study of industrial societies and their social movements that sociology has understood the need to move away from thinking in terms of systems, whether structural-functionalist or Marxist. Actors do not use social institutions only because of their potential to help them achieve a better status in the social hierarchy, but also to strengthen their capacity to undertake social actions as these arise. Manuel Castells demonstrated this superbly in his analysis of Barack Obama's presidential campaign and of the influence of Saul Alinsky on him, providing a solid underpinning to his analytical construct (*Communication Power*, 2009, pp. 386–9).

And Castells adds: 'If structuration is multiple, the analytical challenge is to understand the specificity of power relationships in each one of these levels, forms and scales of social practice and in their structured outcomes.'

## The separation between actors and system

From the beginning of this book, we have highlighted two fundamental elements of the societal type that is taking shape. The first of these is the globalization of the economic system and, consequently, its growing autonomy in relation to actors and institutions. The new society is experiencing an ever deepening rift between an economy which is organized on a world-wide level and institutions or forms of social organization weakened by their inability to control the global character of the economic system. A deep gulf has been created between the economic world and that of social institutions in which there are numerous actors but none capable of controlling the globalized economic world.

For the first time in history, the world of manufacturing, banks and technology has been separated from that of actors. Consequently, actors can therefore no longer be defined by their roles or their status in economic life. This separation marks the end of a very long period characterized by the 'socio-economic' conception of social sciences. In terms of the analysis of systems, economic thought focused on developing formalized analyses of the relationships between the different dimensions of economic life, including those which lie outside the strictly economic sphere. In terms of the actors, we focused our attention on their social role. Today, however, it is no longer possible to analyse actors from this perspective. Indeed, it could even be claimed that this redefinition of actors, as moral and individual actors rather than social ones, is driven by a situation which has itself become non-social, and which commits individuals, groups and institutions to take on the role of defenders (or, on the contrary, opponents) of certain sources of legitimacy. When the separation between system and actors is complete, actors can no longer be defined as social actors given that their legitimacy stems from a higher source. It derives from the fact that they contain within them the subject, or, in other words, rights. This shift should not be interpreted as a transition from a social vision to an approach based on individualism, since this word covers three different types of behaviour arising as a result of the collapse of production-based societies: social breakdown, communitarian behaviour and, finally, the search for new principles of legitimacy defined in terms of rights. The most important of these rights is the right to be an actor, a situation summed up so forcibly by Hannah Arendt, who defined human beings by their 'right to have rights'.

All social categories claim rights. British and American writers even referred to the 'right to be British' in the context of the independence of the British colonies. But it was the French Revolution which brought the notion of rights within general reach. Hannah Arendt explains this by claiming that it was the destruction of all individual rights, as imposed by the Constituent Assembly in 1791, which led to the notion that individuals deprived of their rights, or, in other words, de-socialized, could claim a general – and even universal – right to have rights. Hannah Arendt, influenced by Edmund Burke, develops this argument in the course of her critical examination of the French Revolution and of the French model of democracy. For her, the American model, where the general right to have rights is based on the positive experience of possessing individual rights, is preferable to the French one. One can accept the criticisms made by Hannah Arendt, criticisms already voiced by Tocqueville, while still giving a universalist meaning to the phrase 'the right to have rights'. In contemporary societies even more than in the past, the respect for minorities obliges us to refer to a general right to live according to norms and principles which do not necessarily conform to those of the majority. Yet such a right can only be based on a universal principle.

In any case, the complete separation of actor and system is the very definition of the post-social situation. It shatters all the links previously existing between economic history and social history.

## The absence of a new societal model

The state of crisis which dominates the world economy at the beginning of the twenty-first century, and which is largely the result of the unregulated growth of financial capitalism, is extremely unfavourable to the successful development of a new societal model. Indeed, where such a model emerges, it tends to be in the most modern countries, in the form of non-governmental organizations (NGOs), which also exist in less developed countries where they are largely subsidized by the rich northern countries. Predictably, and in line with all the classic scenarios, a major breakdown in the economic and social system, brought about either as a result of a wave of popular pressure, or at the instigation of political and economic leaders, delays the formation of a new societal type, rather than accelerating it, as one might at first be tempted to suppose. In such a context, social reconstruction, which should encourage new actors to take centre stage, is in fact hindered by the crisis and by the huge reduction in resources. The crisis does not in itself facilitate the modernization of the political and social domain; indeed the opposite is true. And it is only when the crisis sparks off an anti-liberal and even anti-reformist reaction, that any new equilibrium will be reached, paving the way for a global modernization of the kind already in operation in the Scandinavian countries.

Thus the process of change happens in two stages: first economic neoliberalism is overtaken as people's social and cultural rights are extended; then the political monopoly enjoyed by privileged categories of the population comes to an end, leading to a surge of new social and cultural demands and changing the way political life operates.

It is this last point which has recently provoked the most debate. Everyone is conscious of the inadequacy of our *representative* democracy, weakened by the growing social diversification of the industrialized societies. In the United States and in the Commonwealth countries, powerful social and cultural movements have developed, but these operate on another level of political life, a long way from the governmental sphere. The best example of this phenomenon in the

United States, and elsewhere, is the politics of environmentalism, which has rapidly become a significant force in civil society on both sides of the Atlantic.

At the same time, there is evidence of a growing trend on the part of economists to integrate social and political analyses with economic considerations. Amartya Sen is the figurehead of this movement, alongside people such as Joseph Stiglitz, Paul Krugman and Jean-Paul Fitoussi. Once again, new ways of thinking emerge as societal change asserts itself.

### The temptation of a complete breakdown

Our attitude to the void created by the crisis of the industrial societies is *ambivalent*. Some insist that we need to break with the past before we can construct the future; others disagree, and fear that this void may make the creation of new forms of social life impossible, arguing instead that a well-managed process of evolution is essential to the continuity between the old and the new societal type. This second approach has proved to be the shrewder one.

In fact, we need to understand that a serious crisis, even when limited by effective state intervention, can halt progress towards a new type of society or can give it the form of a complete breakdown. The end of the past does not guarantee the birth of a future. Conversely, limited reforms, of a purely technical nature are not enough to change social representations and to mobilize those who expect to be liberated by a new society.

This distinction between a change which involves a smooth transition from past to present, and a change which takes the form of a violent breakdown, or even a revolutionary confrontation, is a classic one. The contrast between the reforms in Great Britain and the upheavals in France is a well-known feature in any analysis of the deep differences between these neighbouring countries.

Continuity makes it possible to select which aspects of the past should be preserved and which discarded, but this can only be achieved through the efficiency of a political system capable of avoiding the all-or-nothing approach, which always comes at too high a cost. A complete breakdown has the major disadvantage of making it all too easy to lose sight of the transformation to be implemented. It can even lead to the creation of an absolute power which severs links with the past, but at the cost of a dictatorship led by whoever is in charge of the breakdown, whether it be an individual or a party.

The current crisis has had negative social consequences without, however, provoking a total break with the past. Democracies have received a great number of blows which have caused damage, though without leading to revolution. In the case of the United States and Western Europe, the crisis has even abolished the notion that a political vacuum inevitably leads to a revolutionary uprising. But it has also caused a division between those two tendencies whose complementarity gives rise to the post-social situation, thereby preventing it from happening. On the one hand, the world of goods and services severs its relations with the social and political institutions and imposes its own laws. But, on the other, the positive process leading to the subjectivation of actors tends to be replaced instead by a process which confines forms of 'spirituality' to the periphery, while an intermediate and largely ephemeral zone is created, in a sense the territory of Erasmus, where the choice between the Pope and Luther never has to be made.

The crisis therefore produces effects which are essentially negative. Globalization and subjectivation form two opposing universes which may even clash with each other at times, and this renders impossible the formation of new actors, new institutions and new negotiations. If the crisis leads to a catastrophe, to a complete breakdown, there is a strong chance that it will favour the formation of a new power in society which will tend to become all-powerful and even totalitarian. The crisis does not bring problems to fruition; instead it brings down not only dead leaves but entire trees.

The most positive aspect of the current crisis could well be that it has helped the United States to heal the very deep scars left by a quarter of a century of uncontrolled liberalism.

The state intervened not only to curb the financial crisis, but also to stem rising inequality. Barack Obama's presidency will be considered a triumph if it were to succeed in stifling the crisis and, at the same time, improving the social policy of the country, something which could never be achieved by any revolutionary breakdown, which, on the contrary, would split society in two by abruptly discarding leaders associated with the past. The logic of violence inevitably obscures and destroys the progress of modernization.

The positive effects of Barack Obama's policy in the United States are limited by the fact that we do not yet know if it will lead to new economic and social policies in the future. Should we subscribe to the idea that this crisis has provoked a change of direction in the United States towards a new Welfare State? Yes, thanks to a major Social Security bill. Across Europe, however, the crisis has tended to result more in defensive policies, or even in confusion and retreat in the matter of social protection.

Of course, it must not be forgotten that continuity exists between one societal type and another, insofar as any society is defined by its level of historicity, or in other words by its greater or lesser capacity to change. For all that, we constantly refer to the incapacity of societies to transform themselves, and not only with reference to countries paralysed by corruption and violence: the examples of France and even more so of Italy are there to prevent us falling for a naively evolutionist vision.

Some people will be disturbed by the term 'post-social situation', but what is still uncertain is the capacity of any particular country or town to mobilize resources, to trust in their own future, to convince themselves that modernization is indispensable to the survival of a country threatened by its more powerful neighbours. Fear does not always lead to success; it is just as likely to lead to violence, distancing society from any new modes of life or action which it could otherwise generate.

We have broken with the idea of progress and this has liberated us from the illusion that progress happens of its own accord: we know that it is more likely to occur when the governing elite are forward-looking and have the means to impose their goals. The country which comes closest to the model of democratic and endogenous modernization is Germany, underpinned by an extremely strong capacity to export its industrial products. At the other end of the scale is China, where the model of modernization depends on decisions made by the Party State, and which therefore cannot guarantee a future characterized by well-being and democracy.

France, too, has experienced periods marked by voluntarism, particularly under the leadership of General de Gaulle, who mistrusted the French and preferred his own idea of France and its future to theirs, a notion which increasingly caused conflict within society, culminating in the clashes of May '68, and which was rapidly abandoned at the time of the first oil crisis in 1974. In fact, it is impossible to be certain whether any given country will or will not move into the post-social situation.

The whole of Europe currently finds itself in the same situation. Ex-Soviet countries are struggling to recover any sense of initiative and rely almost entirely on external aid. Western Europe is split between a minority of modernizers and a majority, dominated by consumers rather than by creators, who want to see a reduction in the place taken by work in their lives, because, for too long, the ruling elite has sacrificed everything else in favour of their personal enrichment. At this point we must leave the economic domain and instead step into that of social science in order to understand that the future depends on the level of confidence that members of a society have both in it and in themselves. Yet this confidence primarily depends on the behaviour of leaders and of governments who do not always realize that when a handful of speculators seize control of common assets, the rest of the population loses confidence in the future of society.

### The three elements of reconstruction

The transition to a post-social situation does not happen of its own accord, as though it were simply a matter of a gradual evolution from one type of society to another. Breakdown always entails a high risk of failure. Those countries which do not succeed in making the leap towards another type of society generally fail, less because of technical reasons but more because of their inability to understand and successfully implement the necessary changes. It is not simply a matter of ignorance. The transition process may be attempted during a period of crisis, of rebellion or against a background of rising inequality. In such cases, it is the rejection of the old regime which is the significant factor and, while this gives the actors involved considerable power, this strength more often tends to culminate in violence than in inventiveness. In these circumstances, a sequence of accidents and errors of judgement is a far more likely scenario than a methodically prepared and successfully executed transition from one type of society to another. For the goal to be achieved is the reconstruction of a vital and active social ensemble, a process which requires a re-definition of the main actors by themselves, a sound knowledge of the enemy to be faced, and an awareness of the common issues which exist between social actors.

– An awareness of the *adversary* is the easiest of these to acquire. For the agents of change come up against resistance from this very adversary, either in the form of defenders of the old order, or of a group of economic leaders imposing their dominance and making excessive profits. This awareness is so easily acquired that it can lead either to conflict or to violence. This outcome can only be avoided if positive self-awareness combines with a critical (or even aggressive) awareness of the adversary to be defeated.

– *Self-awareness* is more difficult to acquire than an awareness of the adversary since the actor is now no longer defined in social terms but instead in universalist, though still very concrete, terms and, above all, in terms of rights rather than of interests.

The new actors *are no longer social* and must now identify themselves with the defence of universal rights. Any difficulty in clarifying the exact extent of the group of actors will be compensated by the radical nature of any new confrontations. The new actors must therefore have a very strong awareness both of their rights and of what threatens them.

At this point of the analysis, the actors defined in 'moral' terms cannot yet be defined by the institutional, and in particular legal, implications of these, since the subject can only come into being outside the realm of social organization. It is a matter of life over death, of rights over interests, of fundamental principles over their consequences.

And this is so true that initially the affirmation of self always takes a utopian form, like that associated with the early days of industrial society when Marx spoke of utopian socialism, which he compared with real socialism. The utopian horizon still beckons to the extent that many young people seek to escape from the real world into an ideal world, in harmony with nature rather than with any type of modern economic organization, which undermines the nascent movement. Young people are attracted to the counterculture. The writings and music which are most popular with young people are very often characterized by a positive self-awareness but also by too vague an opposition to adversaries who are insufficiently defined.

This powerful, even heroic, vision reveals the subject in the individual but nevertheless fails to throw light on a reality which, though more difficult to grasp, is equally important. The individual, now essentially a subject, cannot fulfil his creative role if he is unable to sustain, both in himself and with those who form part of that self, a sense of confidence in his capacity to create. How can someone suffering from self-loathing, denial or world-weariness contribute to the construction of a social space if their determination to be a subject is unable to resist the overwhelming power of the world of money? In industrial societies, it was qualified workers with many years of service in their companies who set up and ran the trade union movements because they needed to defend a genuine autonomy which unqualified and unskilled workers did not have. In the same way, in a society so dominated by a cultural awareness of the self and others, it is those people who seek and value the happiness that comes from being themselves who are best able to construct a new society, for them and for others.

– It remains to define *the issues* at stake in the struggle, issues which are accepted by all but interpreted in conflicting ways by the different sides involved.

In the new situation, in a post-social space and time, what are the issues, what is the main resource over which the opposing sides fight for possession, while still acknowledging that it belongs to everyone? If globalization has destroyed all the institutions as well as society itself, since it is now outside all social control, we are forced to conclude that only *the individual* remains alive in the midst of the ruins.

The liberals, anxious to remove all obstacles capable of hindering the triumphant advance of the market, set out to abolish any sense of belonging, because in their view only individuals rationally seek out their own interests. Their aim is for extreme individualism to wipe out institutions and collective action.

On the other hand, it is also to *the individual* that we turn out of mistrust and hostility towards institutions which have allowed themselves to be exploited by the desire for profit that drives the dominant actors. But the individual, as perceived by those who are dominated, cannot be a subject unless he recognizes that other individuals have the same rights and the same capacity to be themselves subjects. The universalist vision would be meaningless if it served only to bring together individuals and different groups under the shared roof of citizenship, the expression of a sense of belonging which is no longer based on an identity but on equality of rights. Yet, rebuilding a society conceived as a shared house on the basis of the individual-subject and his relationship with other individual-subjects implies an ability to combine a respect for difference with the creation of a universalist awareness of fundamental human rights.

This description is of course far from 'realistic'. It highlights the various ways in which the subject is 'superimposed' on the individual, without, however, having recourse to supernatural forces such as those invoked in voodoo or in the major religions. A necessary, but also deceptive step, like all images of wisdom, of faith and of hope.

The crisis situation precludes happiness. It tears apart and consumes the individual as he seeks within himself the subject, which is the source of his rights. The crisis forces him to turn his back on the subject and instead engage in utilitarian struggles – or even in combats where it is every man for himself.

Yet the more the economic actors are directly affected by the crisis, the more intensely they experience the contradiction between the destruction of the old world and the construction of the subject. The swing of the pendulum between what is destroying the old world and those striving to construct a new one is as likely to result in chaos as to produce a new societal order. Nothing can be more moving than this oscillation, so often impeded by the setbacks and mistakes of those who are determined to stay on the path of subjectivation, but who do not always arrive safely and soundly at their destination. Young people, who are more exposed than others to the temptations of consumerism, and at the same time more affected by unemployment, tend to stray more often than others, losing their way and falling into traps in which they are exploited. Few of them succeed in finding the route which will raise them up and transform them to the point where they are capable of achieving complete subjectivation.

The crisis prevents us from transforming ourselves into subjects. In order to fight off the attacks of enemies of the subject, we must not, however, meet them on their own ground. On the contrary, we must ensure that within ourselves, private consciousness and public action are as closely associated as possible for, in open battle, we are sure to lose everything, whereas the inner fortress can always resist the invasion of private life by utilitarian behaviours.

It is true that there are many more ways to fall than there are to get back up again, but if we strongly sense that the threat of a fall is imminent, we can always get back onto the path which leads upwards towards subjectivation.

These then are two of those moments which have to be faced by all those wishing to participate in the construction of a subject capable of standing up to the massive power of money and of the policies which serve it. The first moment is the one where two paths divide, one leading down to catastrophe and the other leading up towards the subject.

The second moment is the one described in more detail above, in other words the moment in which the elements which constitute the subjectivation of the individual emerge: *self*-awareness, awareness of the *adversary* and a recognition of the *stakes involved* both by those who fall into the abyss and by those who try to construct defences against the forces of destruction, defences constructed not with heavy stones but with high moral standards.

As for the third moment, the hardest of all to describe, this is the one which involves descending from the heights of the subject back into the wide world of social behaviours and relationships. How can we make the transition from principles to concrete applications capable of transforming the space where only the ruins of old institutions are left standing? How can we rebuild institutions, social relationships, organizational systems which will allow the subject to permeate all aspects of social interaction? For it is only as a result of this work at the very heart of society that the subject will be able to create not social bonds, but the potential for each individual to raise themselves towards their own subjectivation and that of others.

# 8

# The emergence of non-social actors

## The logic of pure economics

An economic crisis occurs most often in situations where money is used to make more money rather than to support production. This situation, reminiscent of Marxist thinking, brings us back to the domination of financial and even speculative capitalism over the real economy. In a crisis, there are no social actors in the true sense, since the financiers are defined purely in terms of profit, including speculative profit, whilst all the others, company heads, particularly of small and medium sized companies, and workers, are relegated to the role of victims. For the majority of people, the crisis primarily means unemployment; for several million Americans, it meant losing their homes.

But is there not a tendency for this situation to become widespread and even permanent, with manufacturing facilities switched from one country (or continent) to another and businesses increasingly looking for 'flexibility' (in other words, submission to the demands of the market, not just in terms of jobs but also of every aspect of workers' lives) in order to obtain the maximum profit? Uprooting has been a nodal point of the modern economy ever since the enclosure movement in England, which drove rural workers into the towns. Since then, there have been waves of Germans, Irish, Italians and Spaniards, driven by poverty to the United States or Argentina. More recently Africans, North Africans, West

Indians, but also people from Eastern Europe, have headed for industrialized Europe. In the same way, millions of Hispanics, from Mexico, Central America, Colombia, Ecuador and the Caribbean, have entered the United States.

Many see this uprooting and flexibility as an increasingly general definition of industrialized and capitalist societies and view this influx of people from either a rural environment or an impoverished urban one as normal.

We can speak of societies and institutions in crisis both from the optimistic perspective of the great journey to the West, and from the pessimistic one of the impoverished rural workers uprooted from the Southern States of the United States, whose sufferings were so vividly described by the American author Erskine Caldwell. Modes of production, consumption, trade and research thus transform the world, at the same time threatening the survival of those unable to participate in such transformations. We must also acknowledge the direct consequences of the domination of what Georges Friedmann called the 'the technical milieu' over the natural one. Clearly it is no longer possible to set the natural against the artificial any more than it is to imagine the revenge of man over machine. Nor should technological developments in themselves be seen as a source of freedom, even if Jean Fourastié and others were right to say that the rapid surge in productivity from the end of the nineteenth century onwards resulted in a rise in living standards and a (less rapid) reduction in the amount of time devoted to work. Today, leisure activities are largely dictated by the media, and work in its most modern form is associated with management methods which produce stress levels capable of having a destructive effect on personality.

Work cannot be said to bring either freedom or destruction, for if contemporary society confines us in a tightening web of constraints, it also gives us better and better protection against disease and guarantees us a longer life by keeping at bay the mass poverty rife in less technically advanced societies.

The point of these comments is to emphasize the fact that in the post-social situation, it is no longer in the 'social' or the economic spheres that struggles for freedom are played out. The elimination of one form of domination does not liberate those who were dominated; instead, it paves the way for a new form of 'surveillance', as Michel Foucault puts it, less brutal perhaps but no less restricting. The notion of liberation through work, or indeed through a revolution capable of transforming the social relations of production, makes less and less sense; the truth is that such 'grand narratives', as Jean-François Lyotard called them, have had their day.

This observation can be interpreted in two ways. The first comes down to the idea that man is liberated no longer by work, but by consumption. The proportion of the average lifetime devoted to work has been reduced through shorter working hours, more time spent in education or apprenticeships as well as by an increased life expectancy beyond retirement age. Furthermore, and as a result of all this, it is no longer in the social, and particularly in the professional sphere, that the foundations of freedom and of the responsibility of each individual should be sought. The second interpretation means recognizing the human being as *a creator of symbols*, and therefore involves placing the world of *conscience* and *rights* above society.

We cannot of course claim that the crisis brings us increased freedom, but we are probably justified in thinking that it locks both individuals and a wide range of social categories so firmly into the universe of dominant economic interests, and the destructive effects of economic catastrophes, that it drives them to seek out a non-social basis for their conscience and their demands.

The notion of a purely economic approach, devoid of any particular political or social project, is a clear reflection of what we are experiencing today. The enrichment of the financiers, followed by the collapse of banks and businesses, has led to a crisis in which the vast majority of the population is deprived of any possibility of defending their interests or limiting their losses. As a result, if in the coming months and years certain indicators continue to point to the beginnings of an economic recovery, and in particular to a revival of financial activity, without any corresponding reduction in levels of unemployment, it is possible that a mass reaction of considerable strength (or even of extreme violence) will occur. But this could absolutely not contribute to the affirmation of the new society; it would simply be evidence of the poor organization and the absence of any political project in a population which had fallen victim to the economic crisis.

## The end of the social

The financial actors, who are the only ones with an ultra-rapid capacity for intervention, hold all the cards. In such conditions, we need to look further than the contradiction between the technical and the social organization of work in order to understand the situation in which we now find ourselves, for we no longer live in an industrial, or even a post-industrial, society. The process of transformation is a deeper one which goes beyond the relative decline in industry and in the development of services to people and businesses.

The domination of production and the markets by financiers rather than by industrialists, as in the past, demands a level of analysis which goes beyond a simple understanding of the social relations of production. As a result, the centre stage is occupied on the one hand by a financial economy distanced from the real economy, and on the other by actors who no longer define themselves in terms of an industrial society. It has therefore become impossible to formulate an analysis based on an understanding of the different forms of productive activity and progressing from there to the relationships between classes and finally to their political and even cultural expression. It is this new version of reality which permits us to describe actors no longer as social, that is to say identified by their place within social relationships, but instead to define them in terms of *their relationship with themselves* and with their own personal legitimacy, the latter in opposition to determinants which are increasingly defined in global economic terms.

All these observations are summed up in the expression: the *end of the social*, which refers to the separation between the economic system, over which nobody can any longer claim to exercise any real control, and political and cultural life, which deals with the principles of freedom and of justice rather than the balance of power. Although this expression, the 'end of the social', may seem excessive, it is no less appropriate than it would have been to refer to an 'industrial society' in the eighteenth century, at a time when agricultural production was still playing an important role. In reality, the dynamics of eighteenth-century society, particularly in Great Britain, had already begun to alter with the advent of mass industrialization.

The important thing is that, once the initial shock produced by this expression has worn off, it helps us to grasp the scale of the changes which are taking place. And indeed, they are more profound than those associated with the transition from one stage of industrial society to another. From this perspective, the period of change we are living through is at least analogous to the change from an agricultural to a mercantile society and then to an industrial one. The important point here, as I have made clear, is to recognize that the actors are no longer motivated by their social and economic interests but instead by the desire to defend their *rights*, in other words, to base their desire for freedom and justice on their awareness of the human subject carried within themselves.

In these circumstances, the idea of a central conflict which is strictly social must be replaced by the deeper opposition between the economic world, in all its aspects, and a subjectivity which is increasingly dominated by the direct reference to every individual's right to have their demand for freedom and responsibility acknowledged. The old system, where everyone's behaviour was judged in terms of the functional needs of society, is disappearing. This internal image of the world of social relationships has been replaced by the tension, and even conflict, between the dominant power of the economy and the recognition of the rights of the human subject.

The end of the social results in the transformation of every aspect of collective and private life. And if today the idea of *sustainable development* has become so important, it is because it stems from the clearest realization of the need to rebuild institutions capable of controlling economic life in the name of rights which have a moral basis.

## Beyond the class struggle

The breakdown of the economic and social system and the ever more sharply defined separation between actor and system make it difficult to identify social actors in today's world. This observation will not come as a surprise.

This situation is equally evident amongst the ruling elite and amongst the working population. Liberal economists have stressed the fact that they do not wish any one social category to dominate but simply to ensure that everyone is subject to the rational laws of the market, whilst at the same time recognizing that this domination by the market can have negative effects unless freedom is respected. This idea is an easy one for us to take on board, first because if the economy and the whole of society were dominated by a ruling elite, we would soon hear the loud protests of the dominated. On the contrary, this economic crisis, instead of pushing the population 'to the left', steered it 'to the right', inasmuch as it is left feeling incapable of taking action and hears from both the parties and the unions only declarations which can never be transformed into concrete actions.

Ultimately, it is at the level of government that the two types of demands, those made by management and those by workers, make themselves heard, not directly from one to the other, but both through the medium of this third-party actor which is politics, where what counts most is political influence and an ability to negotiate. Political life is no longer a stage upon which conflicts of interest are translated into political decisions. It is the political field itself which takes the initiative to intervene in these now silent conflicts and to act according to criteria of its own which do not correspond to the interests of either workers or management.

Today, the vocabulary of social philosophy gives considerable emphasis to the notion of *fairness*. This idea conflicts with the principles of economic liberalism, but it also excludes the actors by handing over to the state or to independent experts the responsibility of establishing exactly what constitutes a 'fair' resolution. On this basis, in the past, social movements – workers, feminists or those seeking decolonization – would have found themselves powerless.

The government may decide to prioritize investments or to raise wages, or perhaps to increase the profits distributed to shareholders, depending on its perception of the strength of each actor and, consequently, of the dangers that a crisis may pose for any particular category of actors or for itself. A far cry from the rationalist realism advocated by many economists and business leaders. Such an approach is in fact dictated by the self-interest of a political world intent on minimizing the consequences to itself of a crisis which could lead to either shareholders or the workforce receiving less than their due, or alternatively to inadequate pay differentials between the different grades of workers. This kind of policy is marred by the absence of any clear guidelines upon which to act. Everything is subject to evaluation by the political powers. But, in fact, it is the capacity of the various actors to keep up the pressure that determines the outcome. More often than not, it is the economic and financial leaders, both private or public, that prevail, simply because they are able to exert pressure at the highest level. Conversely, when workers express their dissatisfaction, even when this is largely justi-fied, the government, along with a segment of public opinion, worries about the threats to law and order which might ensue. In these situations, there are no longer any direct links between the actors and the system, and it falls to the state to establish the priorities, in the name of what it esteems to be the public good, thereby further undermining the social actors.

The separation between actors and the system and with it the removal of any underlying working principle, like that of the class struggle in the past, strips the economic system of any possibility of self-regulation. On the one hand, workers have ever wider-ranging preoccupations, for example con-cerning the education and the health of their children or their own earnings, whereas those who have invested capital find themselves increasingly preoccupied with international competition and expect to be compensated for the risks they take or for the benefits they bring to their company as a result of their success in international markets. This reality represents a profound transformation in comparison with the early decades of industrial societies. Whereas, in the past, workers were more easily able to enlist in their favour public funds or public support, now the opposite is true: those whose demands are based on numbers or aggression are less and less likely to achieve their goal. In order to triumph over competitors, it is imperative to be seen to be acting in defence of the common interest – whether economic, social or national. Public opinion calls for state intervention, but governments feel powerless in the face of global capitalism.

### Day and night

Are we now in a position to provide an answer to the question posed at the beginning of this book: how does the economic crisis affect the longer term process of change leading us towards the post-social situation?

The reply to this question can be formulated thus: the crisis accelerates the destruction of society in its previous form, since the social actors are left weakened by it, whereas the non-social actors, such as financial capital on the one hand and the appeal to the subject on the other, acquire a growing importance, in theory limited in both cases by state interventions. But in another respect, the crisis situation means that people are not immediately aware of the changes taking place, since it locks them into the very short term, and in many cases exposes them to personal tragedy, like that which has already affected a considerable number of unemployed people in America, Spain and England, and which is also badly affecting other industrial countries.

And why not combine these two points of view which would appear to be more complementary than contradictory? The positive element of the analysis anticipates the reconstruction of new institutions and laws, and consequently of the social fabric in general. Its negative element is that the individual finds it increasingly difficult to become integrated into both institutional life and economic activity. This is evident from the scale of the illegal or informal economy, which continues to expand as governments struggle to control the growing spread of underground activity. All aspects of economic life are in crisis, and a great many people acknowledge the need to actively oppose this process, while others would settle for tighter social control of banks and businesses.

Only a short time ago, it seemed as though the social integration of the vast majority of the inhabitants of any given country was a real prospect, in particular as a result of a system of social protection, but this hope, at least as far as France is concerned, has more or less faded.

With this in mind, if we compare the current situation in North America and Western Europe with the situation 20 years earlier, we are confronted with an unexpected result published by the INSEE (The French National Institute of Economic and Statistical Information). The gap between the comfortably off and the poor continues to narrow in France, thanks to the Social Security system and to the redistribution of incomes, particularly through taxes. Today it has gone from less than 3.5 to 1, after taxes have been deducted. In contrast, however, certain categories at both ends of the scale are becoming isolated from the rest. The extreme wealth of the higher income earners is easy to spot, whereas the hardship of the poorest people – the unemployed, many elderly people, but also young people and one-parent households – is less conspicuous, although in fact more widespread than official statistics indicate.

In the context of the crisis there is therefore a reinforcement of a general tendency in our societies whereby those at the extremes find themselves further and further away from the mean, while the middle classes and those with stable incomes draw closer to it.

Put a different way, continuing with those existing factors of change specifically associated with the industrial society is proving more and more challenging, and social integration is becoming an illusory objective. In reality, the crisis has increased the proportion of the population who are socially excluded or on the fringes of society.

From a strictly economic point of view, in other words from the perspective of production and of the social relations of production, any prospect of an end to the crisis seems seriously threatened. The fact is that we cannot rebuild the past in a world which has been so severely shaken. Even more than in the past, we now understand that the way out of the crisis will be defined not in purely economic terms but instead in terms of the construction of a new system of actors. But these actors will no longer be social ones, given that some of them, the dominant ones, will now be part of a global economic logic over which no social or political actor can exercise any real control, whereas others, those who find themselves dominated, will turn instead to the notion of a subject which cannot be reduced to a social definition.

## Confirmation of the hypothesis

The hypothesis put forward in chapter 6 seems to be vindicated. This hypothesis in no way seeks to relativize the significance of current global crises, the damaging effects of which will continue to be felt for a long time to come. But it highlights the triumphant rise of religious individualism.

I use the term religious individualism when the principle conferring legitimacy of action is no longer to be found outside the human world, in other words in the domain of the gods, of the future or of myths, but can instead only be found within each human being. The individual-subject takes the place of the individual created by God; it is the subject who exerts the creative role in giving human beings the moral 'sense' of their rights, which includes taking account of the natural or social conditions in which they can be exerted.

The crisis blocks the future, not so much because it would delay crucial innovations, but because it threatens to prevent the development of non-social actors capable of replacing the social actors of the industrial society.

Economic mechanisms are becoming detached from social

behaviour. The champions of socio-economy have led a very positive critical campaign against the naïve optimism of the liberals, which is rejected by many people today. But more important than this critical approach is the disappearance of any truly social actors. Social initiatives are crushed under the weight of economic phenomena. And if the actors can no longer be social, and no longer wish to be, it is because they are changing in nature and in particular with regard to their principle of legitimacy.

The crisis does not cause political awareness to disappear, but it increasingly separates a confused and powerless political life from the sensibilities, initiatives and opinions which are developing in civil society though without yet assuming any organized political form. On the one hand, the enormous weight of the world economy, on the other, protests against the violence of governments, and particularly against the 'inhuman' logic of the global economic order, have allowed hopes of liberation to emerge. But how can new social movements and new types of political institutions take shape if compassion (or anger) cannot be channelled into a certain form of political intervention? Once the transformation of the basic elements of social life has been accepted, it then becomes possible to envisage the reconstruction of collective and personal bonds between the two non-social groups, as opposed to the alternative of radical breakdown. But it is more difficult to imagine how a new image of the human subject could become a central element of the cultural and social landscape. There is not yet a strong enough foundation to support the affirmation of the subject; this process demands a refusal to see human beings reduced simply to their living conditions and to their interests. The notion of the subject contains all that is best in religious thinking and, in the case of Sartre's later writings, in hope, or in other words, in the invocation of a principle, in these cases, which protects in every human being that which is stronger than all forms of power and violence. Basic human rights could not exist unless general opinion rejected any claim by those in power to shape those rights according to their convictions, their interests or their self-styled predictions.

It is clearly impossible to portray our era as one in which human freedom triumphed, given that the twentieth century will always be associated with world war, the death camps, the atom bomb and the mass killings of so many minorities and peoples. But what makes the last century both the most appalling, and yet also the most creative of all, is the fact that what renders human beings 'human' is less and less defined in social terms, to the extent that it is our detachment with regard to our social roles which seems to best enable us to come closest to our humanity and our freedom – a situation which is reflected in the extent of Western interest for all forms of thought and lifestyles which oppose utilitarianism.

These realities should be as easy to recognize as the globalization and internationalization of manufacturing and communication systems. We live in a world of absence, of rejection, of solitude. A refusal to be part of the economic world and a rejection of social obligations often results in de-socialization. But the growing power of the globalized world does not mean there is no scope for action for the subject capable of raising individualism to a truly universalist level. From this perspective, we should no more worship globalization then we should demonize it. Everything hinges on whether we define individualism as the consequence of de-socialization or as a new (non-social) principle of creation.

The important thing is to understand that the crisis can just as easily crush those seeking to build a new world as it can give support to their plans. It is not enough to simply say that the crisis causes social actors to disappear. The entire fabric of our collective life is permeated both by the affirmation of the rights of individuals as subjects and by the destructive effects of the globalized economic system. Our *ambivalence* towards the crisis defines our situation. We have become incapable of making demands, but we know how to escape from the world of wealth and power, which is also that of the crisis. Society, shaken up and destroyed as much by financial games as by certain individual interests, also allows more scope to the expression of personal and collective rights. Even in the most immediate forms of consumption, and especially in sexual relationships, it is possible to have the most elevated experiences both in personal terms and in relation to other people. Conversely, this space where rights can be evoked can also conceal a communitarianism which leads to the rejection of other people. The context of the crisis, with its repercussions not only on the economy but also on society, enables us to see the upheavals and ambiguities of our situation more clearly than in periods of stability.

At a time when our activities and our sense of belonging are increasingly fragmented by changes in social life, the construction of the subject takes place through a reintegration of all these activities within a personal life-project which is based on the determination of each individual to act in a manner compatible with the defence of their personal rights and those of other people.

## Revisiting Soulages

It is no longer possible to believe in the all-powerful nature of progress, in the sun rising to its zenith and spreading its rays across the entire world. Horrific images, whether real or fictional, loom on all sides. The word 'tsunami' has entered our vocabulary, just as our imagination has been taken over by aliens intent on invading and destroying our world or by disaster movies announcing the imminent end of the world.

We find ourselves in the grip of a completely new vision of existence. In the beginning, there was light, created by God (*fiat lux*) and, in this light, we were able to make out objects which were so solid they prompted us to develop an objective representation of our lives. Machines and technology, followed by advances in materials, enhance our lives thanks to the benefits of medicine and of social services, but at the same time threaten them as a result of relations of production which may have pathological effects.

And so the catastrophic predictions come true, economies collapse and as unemployment increases, social exclusion becomes ever more widespread.

But is it perhaps time to overturn the way we think and feel? The *ecologists* were the first to invite us to do so by reappropriating for their own purposes the oldest message of the Club of Rome about the need to challenge the notion of progress. But it is a painter who brings us the clearest message – a message which first struck him in 1979.

Pierre Soulages had already produced a substantial and widely recognized body of work when he discovered the *'outrenoir'* (ultra black), which is, according to him, the art equivalent of exploring another country. He urges us to abandon our attachment to light and to objects to which light gives shape and a sense of objectivity. Instead, he invites us to pass through the wall of black and discover the light reflected on the ridges of black paint covering the canvas. When that happens, we no longer see new objects but instead are caught up in the interdependence of the work, the painter and the spectator. The painting radiates a light which draws the viewer in. At that point we leave behind the world of objects and enter one of images, of depictions and suggestions which are constantly changing depending on the position of the painting itself and on the movements of the viewer as he or she moves around in front of the picture. We have left the world of objectivity behind us and stepped instead into that of subjectivity. Is this not the mirror image of what happens when the social sphere collapses, when the image of a catastrophe towers over us, plunging us into darkness and leaving us in a position which we can only overcome by allowing this world beyond black to take shape within us, a world composed of shadows and lights that convey peace or fear, freedom or imprisonment?

And is what I call the *subject* not simply that perspective that creates sense, in the face of the senselessness of crises, unemployment, totalitarianism or terrorism?

In the face of the darkness which snuffs out light and colour, the ultra black frees the consciousness of the subject by separating it from any social context.

Is it possible to look at the work of Soulages without seeing that it goes beyond the dark tones and the black of Mark Rothko's later years in an exploration of a *beyond* which corresponds to the world of creation?

# 9

# New social and political institutions

## Back to the social

How can a universal principle – the subject, human rights – be transformed into a form of organization and of social relationships? We immediately think of the transition from belief to the Church and of the transformation of the mystical into the political, as Charles Péguy put it, in order to stigmatize those turning their commitment to supporting Dreyfus into a political career. And yet, of course, every step must be taken to avoid this damaging process which would leave society at the mercy of the power of the economic system and open to political manipulation.

The solution to this problem lies in recreating a social fabric where, at the first sign of any threat of such manipulation, not only would a legal barrier immediately present itself but, even more importantly, a reminder to focus on the subject and its rights would be clearly heard.

It is easy to understand why there is so much emphasis on the need to recreate social bonds and why many sociologists see this process as the principal objective of their work. Their dream is to re-establish community-based relationships and to protect all beliefs and commitments except where they cross the boundaries into extremism, intolerance and the arbitrary.

Let us turn the problem around: how can we avoid simply settling for this defensive form of social life, which looks only for peace and security, qualities so fragile that they are equally vulnerable to economic pressure or to the formation of aggressively inward-looking identities? We need to turn to the subject, the only force capable of facing up to the power of the economic world, but which can only be effective if its universalism is transformed into laws and rules capable of halting the triumphant advance of economic egoism.

Instead of thinking about recreating close social bonds we need instead to appeal to a non-social principle which is the subject and which alone is capable of resisting the pressures of profit.

Social relationships and practices must be transparent at all times and the rights of the most vulnerable members of society must always be protected. For some time now, and particularly since the birth of the industrial society, laws aimed at reducing inequalities have been introduced as a result of pressure from the vast majority of the population and with the support of those most open to the idea of the subject. Yet their declarations will prove powerless if they are merely empty words. They will only be given full resonance if those who are dominated appeal to universal principles which go far beyond compassion for the female victims of male domination or for minorities of all types who often find themselves excluded from society or victims of segregation.

It is imperative to defend all those whose rights are denied and whose sufferings are not recognized in a world dominated by production. It is not just a question of equal opportunities; we need to fight against the power of the richest and most powerful. For this superior power is all too often illegally won, through misappropriation of public funds and corruption, through blackmail and the manipulation of both laws and institutions.

There is a generalized need not only for sympathetic groups of neighbours or family reunions where distant cousins can become acquainted, but also for protest groups capable of affirming the most universal principles.

It is no longer enough to invoke a god, progress or a social class in order to combat the anonymous power of money: that can only be achieved through an appeal to the demands coming from the subject, demands which are both individual-ist and universalist. The laws fall into two unevenly weighted categories with some controlling economic life for the benefit of the rich and others defending human rights, justice and freedom from all forms of pressure. It is this second category of laws which needs to be more extensive, better respected and capable of driving back the so-called axiological neutral-ity. But such justice will only prevail if a meta-social principle is carved into the very building blocks of all institutions.

In reality, we are a long way from achieving this, as is evident from the crisis affecting democracy. We wanted democracy to be representative, and with good reason; but it remains for us to identify the interests to be represented and ensure the selection of representative leaders. In this domain we are losing ground, for our societies can no longer be divided into a minority of leaders and an integrated majority of salaried or self-employed workers. We find ourselves increasingly sur-rounded by the socially excluded and by people without job security, and those at the top often owe their position more to their machinations than to the overwhelming success of their businesses. We need therefore to return to the original path of democracy which leads from the bottom upwards. But a renewed participatory democracy is only a first step in the right direction: it will be easier to defend those who have nothing in the name of universal principles, as was demon-strated in the founding texts of American Independence and from the writings of the early months of the Constituent Assembly, and in particular the *Declaration of the rights of man and of the citizen*. It is not, however, a matter of return-ing to the great models of the past. The presence of the subject within the individual does not elevate him or her above others; on the contrary, it commits them to engage with society. The individual-subject defends, both for himself and for others, a zone of freedom thanks to which the indi-vidual cannot be simply reduced to his social roles – and will therefore never wholly be ruled by power.

I am confining myself here to just two examples, both highly significant.

The first of these is the *school system*. Those who defined education as a process of socialization were wrong, to the extent that they contributed in no small part to the loss of individuality, of independence and of responsibility amongst young people. Family upbringing is even more important from the point of view of child development in that it is the dominant influence in the early years. Yet in fact, however great the obstacles in its path, this is more often centred on the child rather than on the acquisition of standards, in contrast to its role half a century ago. All too often school curricula are set by teachers for teachers, and pupils are judged on their capacity to conform to the school rules. The criticism which is constantly directed at this approach is based on the idea that school is above all a means of social selection. The pupils who succeed will be those who accept the limitations of the rigorous professional selection characteristic of French state schools, and *lycées* in particular. A superior social background, coupled with a selective education, critics point out, determines the recruitment of the social and economic elite of the next generation. Moreover, this anti-egalitarian model favours the development of social dynasties and minds more intent on obeying rules than on innovation. This argument, which is by no means recent, for the school system as an instrument of *social selection* is still very much in place, but a more recent idea suggests that the manner of communication between teacher and pupils often has a more significant influence on the results the latter achieve than their social origins. François Dubet demonstrated this very forcibly in France and the effect of this variable is still widely felt throughout the educational system and not only at the cutting edge.

All of which suggests that a solution may be on the horizon. Societies must first acknowledge that their educational systems are producing poor results: a changing world is no longer prepared to submit to fixed and rational rules. Reducing education to simply learning ends up impoverishing and destroying minds in a complex world. The *one best way* defined by Taylor and his followers must be rejected absolutely, both in schools and in workshops.

The French school system is in fact one of the last institutions which is still based on the industrial model of the nineteenth and early twentieth centuries. Yet neither is it possible to defend an educational model which, conversely, would extol the merits of leisure activities and games, since this would favour pupils from wealthier backgrounds who always receive additional support from their families. On the contrary, much more attention needs to be focused on the individual personalities of those involved and on preparing them for life in a world which is professionally demanding but also multicultural. It is therefore not enough to offer a choice between a rigid education and a more flexible one. For both systems may inherently favour those who are best prepared for selection because of their backgrounds. We need to rethink the whole notion of the relationship between pupil and school and abandon the too narrow idea that the principal purpose of education should be to produce good workers and good citizens by means of an intensive application of reason, work and arithmetic.

The second example is that of *work*. Until very recently, it was current practice to ask the same kind of questions about the world of work, in spite of the plethora of publicity promoting self-fulfilment within the working environment. For the transformation of working methods, which has seen the decline of the assembly line, has brought with it new constraints: workers must also respond to the demands of the market and shoulder an appropriate share of the problems faced by the business even though they have no control over their professional activity. Stress, despair and, increasingly frequently, suicide threaten those who are unable to adapt to these situations and the pressures inherent in them. In this area, too, there is an urgent need for change.

## From principle to practice

Let us try to take at least a few steps along the path which leads down from a supra-social principle, underpinning the universalism of human rights – the right to knowledge, the right to respect, the right to be creative. Our task is to identify the conditions necessary for the creation of an economic and institutional order which will above all else respect these universal rights.

The first step involves a genuine recognition of all these rights for everyone, and in particular for the most vulnerable. We must speak here of *solidarity*, for it is this which underpins the recognition of the rights of others, given that all of us have the same fundamental rights. If the very high earnings of some are associated with the poverty of many others, the latter must be guaranteed conditions of security and independence which will allow them to fulfil their role as citizens, including the power to impose heavy taxes on the incomes of the rich – a situation which is the reverse of those types of democracies where only property owners and those with independent means can be citizens.

Complementary to solidarity is *trust*, for this can only be accorded to those who recognize the rights of others, or, in other words, those who recognize a central principle of equality which is, according to Norberto Bobbio's sound conclusion, the principal component of democracy.

Beyond these initial observations, the argument can follow the path mapped out by modern conceptions of democracy. Thus power must stem from the demands of the people, and these must be conveyed to the political world by elected representatives who embody these popular demands. The demands must themselves be formulated in a manner enabling them to be effectively presented. Finally, and most importantly, as the first theoreticians of democracy were quick to realize, the executive power, the state, must be subject to the control of the legislature and the judiciary and, lastly, the electors must be able to give or withhold their support for those who hold political power.

The path which stretches from the principle of fundamental rights to institutions and laws leads essentially via democracy to the conditions of existence that are the same – though in a different form – as those for the overriding respect of basic rights. If we fail to acknowledge that each individual possesses rights which do not have a social origin, since they are universal, then we cannot guarantee that either laws or democracy are respected.

It is this which makes it so difficult to define in concrete terms the conditions and the mode of construction of a new societal model organized around the theme of fundamental rights: the right to knowledge and the right to freedom. For, at each stage, we encounter more limited forms of social reorganization which seem to be self-sufficient and which, for that reason, correspond poorly or not at all with the demands of the new societal model. Nothing demonstrates this better than the notion, so powerful in current sociological thinking, that it is imperative to re-establish the *social bond* – a notion rightly directed against an individualism which would carry within it the destruction of all social organizations and of any trust between actors. Nobody has conveyed this preoccupation as forcibly as Robert Putnam, who, after the publication of *Bowling Alone* in 2000, set up the *Better Together* movement and collaborated with Lewis Feldstein and Dan Cohen on the book *Better Together: Restoring the American Community* (2003). Who could criticize or condemn sociability? Who, apart from a handful of prominent individuals or a few spiritual groups, could consider solitude by its very nature superior to life within a family, a couple or a group? It could even be claimed that the absence of social bonds is an obstacle to behaviours which embrace rights and the universal.

But similarly, a life devoted exclusively to consumption, to self-interest or to the rejection of other people often constitutes an obstacle to what could be referred to as the ascent towards the universal. And the idea that this individualism which excludes others and their rights can be identified with modernity is completely misguided. The search for social bonds is essentially a quest for face-to-face relationships but it should also be pointed out straight away that many advanced forms of behaviour are forged through our relationships with those 'nearest' to us, particularly within the family, even though we need to be wary of behaviour motivated by exalted notions of sacrifice and duty, to the detriment of creativity and of self-fulfilment. Without engaging in more detailed analyses which would quickly extend to most of society, we must avoid setting universalist behaviours against those of a family or professional nature. On the contrary, we need instead to learn how to distinguish an individualism which rejects all forms of social bonds from one which enlists them as the means of achieving its own subjectivation, of recognizing the subject within itself, in other words, that element of universalism which it carries within itself.

## The new political sphere

How has the current crisis affected the creation of a new political environment? Although there have been no major upheavals in this domain, nevertheless a number of anti-cyclical policies have emerged, limiting the consequences of a crisis which would otherwise have produced catastrophic results, as was the case in 1929 and in the following years. State interventions have in fact succeeded in halting what had already been a long period of decline, dating back to the last years of the previous century.

This crisis came not from the bottom, but from the top, and the countries playing the dominant role were the hardest hit. Together with the military failures in the Middle East, it was a contributory factor in the loss by the United States of its hegemonic domination over the rest of the world. It is no longer possible to portray the United States as the armed defender of 'western values', as was the case when George W. Bush was in power. The future of American power will henceforward depend on how it conducts itself and on the intentions of other countries, especially those who themselves aspire to a certain degree of hegemony. The growing influence of these major emerging countries means that it is no longer relevant to depict the world as a pyramid made up of countries in varying stages of development with the United States in pride of place at the top.

Criticism has come from all sides of what Immanuel Wallerstein called 'European universalism'. The term has in fact two distinct meanings. It is an unfortunate but indubitable fact that the West viewed the entire world and its history as an ascent towards the universal that they alone had reached, and this conception has reduced the other nations to the role of pupils – and often poor pupils at that. The identification of a particular country or civilization with the universal must always be rejected for it amounts to confusing modernity, which is one and universalist, with the many different routes leading to it, amongst which those chosen by the West are in no way superior. It is true that those in the West, largely through the influence of Christianity, have long separated the spiritual from the temporal, and have consequently introduced a reference to the universal which opened the breach to the philosophy of the Enlightenment and then the philosophy of history (seen as the march of progress). On the other hand, if the social and political aspects of Western history can indeed be criticized, such as its claims to an *absolute* universal, it is clear that modernity could not exist without the adoption of 'universalist' thinking. But others may view things differently.

In addition to Western societies, many others are similarly locked into the notion of their own superiority over all others. This represents a mirror image of the one I have exposed above. These societies refuse to separate universalism from their own particular existence, which may sometimes even be presented as an expression of a divine choice. Such claims must be rejected.

### The revenge of states

At first sight, nothing seems simpler than to foresee the development of institutions, many of which already exist, that would be capable of intervening at the highest level of the globalized economic and financial world. But reality has crushed any such hopes. Economic globalization has not led to political globalization. American and Japanese mass culture is spreading worldwide, especially amongst adolescents, but there is more evidence of older cultural conventions being wiped out than of a new culture being created. The distance between 'globalized' elites and the rest of the population continues to grow.

This is even truer when it comes to language for, particularly amongst young people, the dominant language has become that of SMS, a system better adapted to expressing facts and feelings rather than more abstract ideas. Yet while these new realities affect everyone, they are not indicative of the creation of new content, but much more about the destruction of certain old conventions.

As for the notion that we are already part of a *globalized society*, experience within Europe indicates that, to say the least, this remains to be confirmed. And the same conclusion applies to other parts of the world too.

For a long time, Europeans, at least those in Western Europe, took a pro-European stance with a view to bringing an end to the conflicts between nations which had destroyed Europe and to creating an economic entity comparable with that of the United States, or even of China and India. This belief in Europe was strongest in Germany, based as it was on the country's rejection of nationalism. It was further supported by the writings of Jürgen Habermas and by the speeches of Daniel Cohn-Bendit. But who today refers to the 'Constitutional patriotism' urged by Jürgen Habermas, when Europe struggled to adopt a Constitution, even one limited to administrative and economic measures? The financial crisis has robbed the European idea of much of its strength and we are witnessing the return of national policies, though these have not led to any new form of protectionism. This has so far been avoided by the major Western powers, protecting them from an even greater catastrophe.

In the face of this out-dated attitude within Europe, we have seen a genuine weakening of national cultures. At the same time, national languages have been marginalized by English, which became *the* language of advanced technology and international gatherings. Both the press and the entertainment media have made us more and more familiar with the American way of life and mass culture has meant that not only westerns and gangster films but also Marilyn and Woody Allen have become ubiquitous. We have even seen that some citizens of major European countries attach ever diminishing importance to their own nationality, so convinced are they that the concept of nationality no longer has any reality. This attitude reached an extreme when patriotism appeared to apply exclusively to football. Even then, in the majority of cases, it had more to do with patriotism founded on allegiance to a club rather than to a nation, and even the least informed person was well aware that the teams in question were made up of players who were often foreign, such as Brazilians and Africans.

When the crisis hit the international financial system based in London and New York, any concept of a globalized society vanished.

If Americans play an eminent role in the fields of science and technology, as well as in the arts and in literature, it must be remembered that these sectors involve only a small percentage of the North American population and that the rest live very differently and often within very limited horizons. And is it not striking that President Obama, who in spite of the predictable erosion of his popularity still enjoys very strong support outside his own country, should be the first American president not to have European origins and the first to be so openly critical of European leaders?

It remains to add that in political and cultural terms, as in the economic world or in the matter of military commitments, it is no use expecting Europe to take steps which might lead to the establishment of more egalitarian relationships within the Western world. The European Commission increasingly sees itself responsible for the successful integration of Europe within the global economy and in the context of an international political scene dominated by the United States. It is true that certain European countries are beginning to distance themselves. Germany takes the lead here, with its determination to preserve its export policy at the expense of its own population and of its neighbours, and its tendency, since Schröder became chancellor, to begin looking towards Russia. France similarly, although very open to American culture, remains hostile towards its policies, and opposed the war in Iraq with strength and conviction for reasons which turned out to be justified.

How can a community fail to react to finding itself relegated to insignificance in global terms? Given the enormous attraction which the United States still exerts, there is of course a scattering of individuals or small groups, particularly professionals, who actively seek integration into the American sphere. But the internationalism of economic leaders fails to reflect what their populations feel about this subject. On the contrary, we are witnessing a revival of national consciousness, initially in countries which were formerly colonies, or in ones long since freed from Spanish domination. Central and Eastern European countries, for their part, began by rebelling against Moscow. The national dimension of their action had widespread significance, even if, from Budapest to Prague and from Prague to Gdansk, the liberation movement was also associated with the workers' movement which had been swallowed up under Communist rule and which allowed itself to be swept along by the desire to re-establish links with a West to which it felt it belonged. Likewise Yugoslavia, created and controlled by the Serbs, found itself transformed into a bloody battleground, and even within Bosnia, Serbs, Croatians and those we refer to as Muslims tore each other apart in the name of a nation, a religion and a culture.

In other countries, conversely, we have seen states disintegrate or disappear. This is particularly the case in Central America, and more precisely in Salvador, a country torn apart by a long civil war, a severe economic crisis and open conflict between two main factions, the *maras*. These both started life in Los Angeles, amongst Mexican and Salvadorian immigrants, and they maintain a regime of violence whilst to some extent taking on the role of the state. But beyond these dramatic cases, there is no sign that nations are currently showing any signs of being absorbed into the realm of supranational organizations.

### New actors

Let us now focus our attention in the opposite direction and turn away from globalization to those forms of action which

are replacing the activities of groups representing social interests, legitimizing their actions on the basis of an appeal to the
subject and challenging the effects of globalization, a process
itself situated beyond the reach of society and therefore
outside its control.

We have just seen that the nation state, which we expected
to be superseded, is indeed losing some of its capacity to act
but, conversely, is effectively strengthened by the desire of
each nation or each region to protect itself against the consequences of the global crisis and to safeguard its past, its herit-
age, its language and its collective memory. The problems
posed by the introduction of a moral principle embodied
in the subject are clearly of a very different nature to those
caused by globalization in terms of national identity. How can
this universalist principle permeate specific social situations?
For it is obvious that in the highest reaches of society, that is
to say at the level of governments, any moral and philosophical discourse goes unheard, and that, amongst the population
in general, such views provoke negative reactions by virtue of
their inability to bring practical and rapid responses to those
in the grip of fear and suspicion.

Within civil society however, far from the centres of political and economic power, such views meet with an altogether
warmer welcome and can give rise to the formation of collective action based on protecting human rights, particularly for
the least privileged.

Certainly, at a time when women have become the principal actors in social transformation, it is clear that the crisis
has led to a certain withdrawal into family life, as professional
prospects diminish or disappear altogether. For a period
which they hope will be a limited one, many women prefer
to prioritize family life and in particular their children, at the
stage when these are most vulnerable. Women rather than
men tend to withdraw into family life, insofar as, in the vast
majority of cases, men are still paid more than women, and
traditional stereotypes still tend to confine women to the
home. Although there is no evidence of a genuine change of
attitude in relation to work, there is certainly a lack of confidence in the possibility both of finding work and in the likely

working conditions which might have to be faced, among which the possibility of enforced geographic relocation is a significant factor. But this reaction is not significant enough to overturn deep-rooted tendencies.

When employment problems became more urgent and more widespread, from the second half of the nineteenth century onwards, trade unions, confederations and political parties were set up to organize the struggle to defend workers' rights. Today, the reverse is true, as the slow but already significant reduction in industrial activities as a share of overall activity, the result of outsourcing, relocation abroad and competition from emerging countries, is reflected in the generalized decline of the trade unions.

However, in a less organized manner but at all levels of society, a considerable number of movements are emerging, the majority of which proclaim *cultural* aims inspired by environmental concerns in the face of the blindness of the economic system, notably with a view to protecting the environment and the climatic conditions essential to our survival. These grass-roots movements call attention to the rights of minorities as well as to those of humanity as a whole. In many of them, women play a more significant role than was the case in political parties and trade unions, for all these groups have cultural objectives that can only be achieved through a conviction that an economic point of view must be compatible with environmental factors and with a respect for the fundamental rights of everyone. The disasters which scientists have warned us about would be unavoidable were there not evidence, on a worldwide scale, of changes in patterns both of production and consumption.

The crisis did not in itself provoke the formation of such movements, but by weakening industrial and post-industrial societies and casting uncertainty over their future, it prepared the ground for the development of new forms of collective action. The more the economy finds itself ruled by the irresponsible adventures of financial capital, the more the predictions of inevitable catastrophe will turn out to be tragically accurate. Yet, as early as the end of 2009, at the time when the banks were experiencing a spectacular recovery, which did not, however, signal the end of the crisis, financiers were turning ever more enthusiastically to 'derivatives'. How could this new assault by financial capital fail to bring in its wake an accelerated maturation of movements whose principal objective is the preservation of fundamental rights for all human beings?

However, such action still needs to be properly organized and supported by institutions, which brings us back for a moment to the question of the silence of the victims. As long as the crisis threatens and disrupts the lives of the vast majority of people, it is difficult for them to organize themselves, given that everyone's first concern is to protect their own interests and those of people closest to them. Almost everywhere, the decline of the parties of the left resulted in the interests of the most privileged groups being protected, but this paradox should not be expected to last forever. A conjunction of general problems and events capable of acting as an abrupt wake-up call for public opinion could bring about the rapid downfall of a government which had seemed all-powerful only moments beforehand.

The fragmentation of society ended up destroying the social actors, a process which not only favoured isolated and socially excluded individuals, but also, just as importantly, enhanced the capacity of each individual or each group to discover a new legitimacy within themselves. With one reservation however: this awareness of human rights can only be attained insofar as society has considerable capacity to transform itself, in other words if it is endowed with a strong sense of *historicity*. Where this is not the case, this recognition of the subject is indirect rather than direct and must function through the intermediary of religious belief, through the sanctification of society or even through recourse to a philosophy of history in accordance with which evolution should lead to the triumph of a nation or a class. In fact, in all types of society, from the most advanced to the most fragile, there will be obstacles and wrong turnings which will hinder that society's ability to recognize its own creative capacity and, even more importantly, to proclaim the right of each individual to be recognized and respected as a subject.

## Europe rejected on two sides

The current European Union was initially created to bring an end to the wars which had brought the continent to its knees. Very quickly, however, its goals, and indeed its whole raison d'être, became largely economic ones. It was a matter of adapting European countries to the major economic and political entities that were forming throughout the world. It might therefore have been expected that, faced with a serious economic crisis, the European Union would demonstrate its superiority over individual states. Yet the European idea had long since lost much of its strength. The reality was that the construction of Europe had proved difficult. Amongst the new member countries, the former Soviet republics entered Europe with more suspicion than hope. Poland, still wary of a possible Russian attack, counted more on the United States for military support than on Europe. For their part, those countries who were already members of the Union only agreed to accept a constitutional system after a number of failed attempts and following a challenge to the original text which defined the respective powers of the European Union, of the Parliament and of the Commission.

Faced with the banking crisis and the risk of a total collapse of the financial system, the European Union did not play the leading role. Furthermore, right from the time it was set up, Europe had avoided giving itself any powers, either civil or military, to intervene in world events. Nevertheless, various armed contingents from a number of European countries, including Germany, took part in a military intervention in Afghanistan. (A different situation, it should be emphasized, from that of the war in Iraq, in which a number of European countries, such as the United Kingdom and Spain, took an active part, eventually overthrowing Saddam's government.) Be that as it may, both public opinion and the political parties agreed that the internal problems of each country should not be placed in the remote hands of the European Union. Moreover, the diversity of circumstances, from West to East and from North to South, naturally tends to confer a greater autonomy onto individual states.

The weakness of the European Union has created a paradoxical situation. Continental Europe has suffered the effects of a crisis provoked by the City and by Wall Street. But these two super-powers, supported by India and the oil-producing countries, intervened in Copenhagen to slow down projected agreements on climate protection, in spite of the fact that the United States and China are the two largest polluters in the world. In the meanwhile, Europeans have learnt to limit their energy consumption and to swap the bath for the shower in a gesture which, given the scale of China's coal consumption, seems almost risible. It would appear in fact that Europeans have been urged both to make sacrifices and to sit back and accept everything rather than take any initiatives, leaving the newly emerging countries and the United States to assume control of the world that will emerge once the various crises are over.

In reality, the economic crisis forces the European Union to confront an extremely significant choice. Faced with the very rapid rise in the power of China, and a similar, though slower rise in that of India, as well as of Brazil, all the Western countries, both Europeans and North Americans, find themselves considering the best way to protect themselves. Does this lie in accelerating the integration of the Western world under American leadership or, alternatively, in replacing the existing system with *a more egalitarian relationship* between the United States and the European Union? The notion of a Europe claiming equality with the United States disappeared from our political horizon long ago, and as far back as the 1970s General de Gaulle seemed to have little support either among the chancellors of Europe or within the Commission itself. But these ideas are once again taking centre stage, and not just in France, and a few, still admittedly isolated, voices have already spoken out in favour of an Atlantic Alliance based on a balance between the United States and Europe. Perhaps it is already too late for this and the European Union is merely the shroud of a now ghostly Europe. Yes, Europe is indeed the principal victim of the current crisis, but it is also responsible for its own weakness.

## The failure of the Rhine model

The current debate cannot focus only on economic matters and on identifying protection against any further crisis; it must also deal with military and diplomatic issues since it is above all important to establish whether Europe is indeed capable of claiming for itself a significant role in world affairs. In practical terms, is Europe in a position to put forward an original approach with regard to the Muslim world, one which would at any rate be different from that adopted by the United States towards the Arab world? With this in mind, it might be supposed that Europe would choose to turn first to those countries which have never been colonized by the Europeans and which traditionally have enjoyed a strong state apparatus. The country which best fits this description is of course Turkey. Yet it is common knowledge that certain European countries oppose its entry into the European Union and that the French president's hostility to this newcomer represents an additional difficulty since many countries are reluctant to openly oppose France. This can therefore only happen as part of a long-term process, even if it seems likely to succeed in the end. Looked at optimistically, the choice of an international policy of this sort could even have decisive effects on Iran, a country which corresponds to the two criteria cited – given that it has only ever been colonized by Turkey. It might also, and even more importantly, be supposed that Europe might well be inspired to play a more active role in the search for a resolution to the conflict between Israelis and Palestinians. All that is a long way ahead and, while nobody would wish to see the failure of the European project, it must nevertheless be recognized that Europe has done more to redistribute the wealth of Western European countries across the rest of the continent – from Spain, where modernization was a great success, to the ex-communist countries – than to provide Europeans with the means of making themselves heard in the world at large and of playing an important role on the international stage.

In his study of the post-war period, when economies and states were being rebuilt, Michel Albert identified two opposing models of economic policy: a Rhine model and a liberal (or Atlantic) model. The Rhine model turned out in fact to be composed of two different models. On the one hand, there was the Franco-German one, based on an advanced social policy, aimed primarily at combating inequalities and, on the other, the Scandinavian model, much more socially active though at the cost of an onerous fiscal policy, but able to guarantee individuals very significant social benefits while still maintaining a strong position in the world economic order.

The transformation in European politics from the 1970s onwards can be summed up in terms of the decline and loss of influence of the Rhine model, and the corresponding expansion of the Atlantic model, backed by the United States and favoured by the ex-communist countries who have always placed their trust in the American army.

During the last quarter of the twentieth century, we indeed saw a growing imbalance taking shape between the two main partners, America and Europe. In Europe, the decline of the various 'workers' parties, starting with the communist and then the socialist parties and followed by the radical minorities and, then more dramatically still, by the trade unions after the decisive defeat inflicted on them in Great Britain by Margaret Thatcher, resulted in a significant reduction in projects associated with the 'left'. In France, unionization has virtually disappeared within the private sector, with the exception of a few very large companies, and has retained its strength only in the major public sector companies. The growing weakness of this actor with both trade union and political affiliations has hampered the intervention of the European Union, which, on the contrary, has made its prime aim that of making Europe globally competitive by adopting the (conservative) idea of prioritizing the destruction of all obstacles to a development stimulated by the removal of economic borders.

Public opinion was not mistaken; its support for the European project has, for this very reason, continued to deteriorate. All the major European countries have refused to move towards a federal model and the supporters of economic integration are right to point out that this target is a long way from being reached, particularly in regard to budgets, and therefore in terms of social policies. The long evolution, which had seen Western Europe move from a socially violent industrialization to the social policies introduced under the influence of unions, has finally been turned on its head. In the course of the last quarter of the twentieth century, the liberal model, that of the United States and of Great Britain, has won out over the others, and all the more comprehensively because the organizations representing workers had themselves been weakened, particularly as a result of the radicalism of the most active sectors but also because of the opposition by many companies to any form of negotiation.

Another European weakness lies in the fact that businesses, especially in the Latin countries, did not take a sufficient share of the indispensable costs represented by research, higher education and technical innovation, all of which should in reality be seen as investments rather than as costs. This weakness is particularly noticeable in a country such as Spain, which has, however, made an admirable comeback. In France, the capacity to get long-term projects off the ground has declined steadily, and our country is partly living on the inheritance of the Gaullist period and its major initiatives. The creation of a single currency to which a large number of countries, with the exception of Great Britain, signed up, had the advantage of eliminating any possibility of a policy of competitive devaluation. But this corrective option did not produce quite the desired result: additional measures were needed. And it is no coincidence that Great Britain and Sweden, who are not members of the Eurozone, have obtained better results than those countries who are. Of course these weaknesses in terms of the Eurozone and any action undertaken by Europe can always be rectified by new economic policies, but this threatens to be more and more difficult in that the growing weakness of Europe has resulted in a powerful rise in the xenophobia which, following an upsurge in France with the National Front party under Jean-Marie Le Pen, has since spread to a large number of European countries, with the fortunate exception of Germany.

Corporatist resistance has also contributed to undermining the capacity of European countries to adopt a more active policy in the cutting-edge sectors. But the most decisive factor in this delay will certainly have been the reluctance by Europeans to construct a policy directed towards the future. Europe clearly prefers to build museums which will attract tourists than laboratories and technical centres of excellence which will improve its capacity for innovation and production. It is therefore difficult to see how, over the course of the coming years, the current crisis could cease to act as a brake on modernization.

It might, however, be supposed that Europe, or what perhaps in the present circumstances it would be more accurate to refer to as the Eurozone, must today acknowledge the urgent need to develop a far greater capacity for collective action than that with which it had been satisfied since its inception. Opposition to the Maastricht Treaty, which had triumphed, particularly in France, can now only signal the end of the Eurozone. It is true that surges of protectionism or nationalism mixed with economic protectionism and xenophobia have sprung up in many places, with the Scandinavian countries being particularly susceptible. But it is unlikely that the major countries would risk cutting themselves off and exposing themselves to the predictable reactions of countries which would feel threatened by any unilateral decision to devalue.

In the second phase of the Greek crisis, the Eurozone decided at the last minute, and in spite of considerable reticence from both Germany and the Christian Democratic Union (CDU) itself, to set up a major sovereign loan guarantee fund. But many economists immediately reacted to this by pointing out that these reserve funds should have been much bigger because there was a strong likelihood they would need to respond to crises potentially involving sums of up to 2000 billion euros. Indeed, in the middle of 2011, we saw aggressive speculative financial operations targeted at Italy, where the political situation seemed extremely fragile and even, with far less justification, against France, where admittedly at least two major banks were heavily involved in the Greek economy.

Such crises have focused attention on the creation of Eurobonds, which would introduce a much greater solidarity between the member states. But this project is still meeting strong opposition in Germany. Moreover, Germany continues to send out ever stronger signals of its desire for economic independence. This was particularly evident in its abrupt and unilateral decision, in the wake of the Japanese disaster at Fukushima, to abandon nuclear energy production, a decision which at least for a long period of transition will force the country back on more polluting sources of energy such as gas or even coal.

As it is impossible to predict with any certainty how the French position will evolve in the aftermath of the 2012 presidential and legislative elections, we are forced to the conclusion that Europe, having weighed up the dangers threatening it, may not yet have sufficient confidence in itself to take a decisive step towards economic, and especially financial, integration.

It can only be concluded that Europe – as the Eurozone – although increasingly aware of the need to take steps towards deeper integration, remains as yet unsure about its readiness to effectively embark on transformations which will have repercussions on all aspects of life across the continent.

## A committed search

But, once again, there can be no question here of favouring the reconstruction of social democracy or, at a more psycho-sociological level, of social bonds. Such a prospect belongs more to the past than to the future, and the best that could be hoped for would be to halt the decline of Social Security and the funding cuts affecting hospitals and universities. Nor is it a matter of rebuilding a society starting with relationships based on families, friendships, neighbourhood and so on upwards thanks to a wider participatory democracy. Those who defend the argument for the creation of new social bonds render a service to society but within very narrow limits, since they seek no further than an analysis of social life which simply situates it on the integration–disintegration axis, an extremely simplified version of classic sociology. Yet it is from a completely different starting point that we need to approach the analysis and define any possible action. The only effective resistance to the domination exerted by the globalized economic world is indeed to appeal as directly as possible to the subject, that is to say, to the fundamental and universal rights of human beings. We need to take defensive action on every level, and, even more importantly, to launch a counter-offensive.

From this perspective, it is not a question of organizing action on a huge scale, but instead individual or collective activities in which each individual is *committed* without being integrated. Far from adherence to a group, it is *exemplary* behaviour that is important. This is why small, exemplary, utopian communities play an important role whereas communitarianism is always dangerous. The individual or the group only has a positive role if it carries within itself the reference to the subject, and that in the most direct way possible. And there is no danger of this sliding into moralism given the serious risk of a new economic and social crisis: such conditions leave no place either for selfish isolation or for any indifference to the need to defend rights which are constantly under threat.

Some people are alarmed at the choice of such values and warn against the danger of moving away from objective analysis. No one would deny the potential danger inherent in reducing the sociologist's analysis to a list of opinions and views of human life. But it is not enough to be objective; we must be able to recognize the value judgements which guide the actors, especially in the period immediately following an era dominated by totalitarianisms. Who could speak 'objectively' about the Holocaust? Only an absolute rejection of Evil makes it possible to understand what that was, how it came about, why it was allowed to continue – and why a number of those who were aware of the existence of the death camps chose to remain silent.

Those who claim to be unaware of the idea of the subject, or who reject it, are endeavouring to blind those who need to look more intently in order to denounce all the ways in which fundamental rights are being destroyed.

# Conclusions

The crisis which erupted on 24 October 1929 remained unre-
solved. Germany was the first country to emerge from it due
to the policy of rearmament and mobilization instituted by the
Nazi regime from 1933 onwards. During the 1930s, a major
social movement in the United States and in France meant
that both countries were, after a long delay, finally able to
bring their social policies up to date, but the United States only
emerged from the crisis when it entered the war. The cow-
ardice demonstrated by Great Britain and France at Munich
encouraged Hitler to launch the Second World War in 1939.
It is therefore politics rather than economics that governed
the fate of the major industrial countries. Japan, already mili-
tarized for some considerable time, was engaged in wars of
conquest in Manchuria and Korea and had annexed Taiwan.

What we refer to as the current crisis, which erupted in
2007 and reached its most dangerous peak in September
2008, did not, thanks to President Obama, turn into a generalized, systemic crisis of the Western or even the world
economy, but the underlying causes of the crisis were not
eradicated. The banking sector quickly recovered its prosperity, while the economies of nations, and in the first instance
of Iceland, Ireland and Greece, were threatened with collapse
which was only avoided through the intervention of the main
European countries and the IMF. At the end of 2010, while
most continents were experiencing strong growth, Europe
seemed condemned to stagnation.

The book you have just read presents a view of the current crisis which, though certainly less dramatic than that of 1929, is more alarming and even more difficult to overcome. This is because the effects of this crisis are multiplied by the effects of financial and economic globalization which destroy all the links between the economy and society. All chance of an 'internal' solution to the crisis has gone; it can no longer be overcome through reforms and a tighter control of financial operations.

There appear to be only two possible ways out of the crisis: one via catastrophe, at least within Europe, and the other through the creation of a new social fabric, based not as in the past on the redistribution of national income, but on the affirmation that the defence of universal human rights is the only possible weapon against the clear victory of the globalized economy. This notion, which seems to belong to the realm of pure imagination, must on the contrary be taken literally. All social institutions must be rebuilt to serve the subjectivation of the actors and to save the planet, rather than in the interests of profit. Everyone senses that the task is immensely difficult and the risk of failure very high, but also that the terms I use indicate the only positive solution to a crisis which goes beyond the workings of the economy in that it is occurring in a world where all links between economy and society have been severed by a globalization of the economy which nobody can any longer control.

This last sentence carries within it the conclusion of this study. For the most important long-term transformation in economic and social life is the substitution of conflicts between social actors (which we may call classes) by a con-tradiction between the economic system, particularly when it is driven by purely financial objectives, and actors who are opposed to the reign of money in the name of principles which are more moral than social (such as the right of all individuals to life, security, freedom) which must be pro-tected or revived.

In focusing on the globalization of systems of produc-tion or even of capitalism, we have already emphasized the separation between the way systems function, transformed by new communication technology, and the behaviour of actors, which implicitly always involves time to reflect, make choices and establish direction. Social actors fear that crises will eventually destroy social life, to the extent that, even armed with powerful technology, people will have no control over these crises because economic systems bring into play forces which leave no place for the views and interventions of human beings. The more the rift between the objectivity of natural sciences and the constant appeal made by human and social sciences to subjectivity, and to subjectivation above all, widens, the more the space, which separated but at the same time united them, becomes devoid of content. The notion of society is destroyed. Its disappearance involves the complete separation between the analysis of systems and that of behaviours and of social representations: it is no longer possible today to apply anthropomorphic interpretations to social systems.

This breakdown need not be perceived in its most extreme form. It could well be that the notion of society will not disappear completely, any more than does a city destroyed by bombs. The last two centuries have increased the pressure that natural sciences exert on human and social sciences, particularly when, as Edgar Morin pointed out, these resort to forms of scientific thought which are already outdated. But neither of these sciences is able to stand up to the transformation in scientific thought.

We must agree to travel along two opposing paths: one which leads us to the discovery of the increasingly complex mechanisms at work in nature, including human nature, and the other to all the efforts which together have led to the creation of increasingly dynamic social actors, ranging from the importance accorded to interactions and to forms of collective control within the economy, up to the quest for the individual or collective subject through political behaviour. This separation between subject and system, which can be summed up as the disappearance of the *social actor*, has, since the century of Enlightenment, gone hand in hand with appeals to the subject which today are no longer addressed to a *social subject* but to a *personal, moral subject*. At the end of the twentieth century, much of which was dominated by wars between totalitarian states, we avoid like the plague any association between science and political ideology. Actors are less and less defined by their social affiliations and instead are increasingly committed to the notion of the subject. This is defined as the capacity of human beings to take on the responsibility for their own rights, a state achieved through language, works of art and through the creation of a 'beyond' – seen as the origin of their own creativity. Our material and intellectual undertakings demonstrate with increasing clarity the separation in human life between the world of facts and the world of rights, and help us understand that the principle legitimizing our behaviour lies within ourselves, that it stems from our capacity to create a world in which rights are valued and respected and to protect it from attacks by inhuman systems.

Today therefore we can clearly see the separation between objective economic mechanisms and the defensive moral and cultural principle whereby actors are able to look within themselves and to reflect on their rights, thanks to the human capacity to modify their situation, and thus reach a more or less direct representation of the subject, which transforms the individual or the group from a physical being to one endowed with rights. Between these two opposing movements, which have often clashed, the intervening zone, defined by our predecessors as the social realm, is emptying. The twentieth century left in its wake more social ruins than new constructions. Talk of breakdowns and of crises in no way implies that what the future holds is revealed at any specific moment. Which is why, from the very beginning, I pointed out that the subject of this book was the *interaction* between a *crisis*, which begins on a precise date, and the long-term *transition period*, which eventually gives rise to the *post-social situation*. We constantly need to see ourselves in the context of an ongoing story.

In pre-modern societies, the techniques and forms of government were often inextricably linked to a religion or to a family-based organization. Today these two orders of reality have become almost completely separate and the human population champions a conception of human rights which opposes the violence inherent in any union of temporal and spiritual power, of a technical system and a vision of the world. In fact, when we are not submerged by a wave of totalitarianism, we are living a double experience with, on the one hand, our rapidly expanding knowledge of nature and, on the other, our respect for human beings, in other words for the universal rights of each individual in their capacity as a subject.

Yet let us be completely clear that on both sides, that of personal rights as well as that of complex systems, there are negative tendencies. And it is because we know this that we no longer believe in progress. The advances in modern science can just as easily be used to make war as to make peace; in the same way, the appeal to an identity, which implies a respect of the differences between human beings, can also mean reducing them to their biological, ethnic or religious affiliations. The era of wars between nations is receding, at least in Western Europe, but it has not disappeared completely. Wars between empires have diminished in importance since the destruction of the Soviet Empire, yet at the same time we sense all around us new ways of denying the existence of the Other and of his or her rights. Let us take advantage of current anxieties in order to increase our awareness of what it is that allows us to claim both individual and universal rights. This task is vitally important given that for two centuries the capacity to create within, each individual, something which goes beyond the individual had been rejected and seen as a target for persecution, in the name of a material and political power which is more prompt and ready to take up arms than our individual consciousness of the subject we carry within us.

There is no clear-cut division of Good and Evil between the two sides. This powerful and solitary word: the subject, allows an equal communication between individuals and communities who are ready to acknowledge either directly, or through technical, social and cultural differences, the unicity of the subject, which cannot be infringed by the diversity of identities and by their relationship with power and beliefs. But failures and set-backs are evident on both sides.

We know all too well that the idea of the concrete unity of men and of societies can justify conquests – and even mass destruction. Fortunately, it will soon be impossible to defend arbitrary ideas such as the superiority of West over East, of North over South, or even of one language over another, or one religion over others. Ecumenical movements, which enjoyed an important revival under Pope Jean-Paul II, will no longer see their goal as that of bringing the diversity of the various churches into one single faith or one Church, but simply that of allowing each religious community the space to best combine its own singularity with the universalist character of principles common to all religious faiths, all secular conceptions of progress and all forms of tolerance.

There is no other route towards tolerance and peace except through the recognition both of the *unicity* of the principles which define the human subject and the extreme *variety* of paths along which each community is transformed. The paths of modernization lie further and further apart from each other, but they converge towards the same fundamental affirmations and towards the desire to combine the unicity of modernity with the plurality of those paths leading to modernization, even if they do not always reach it.

This reminder of such simple statements leaves a large void in our collective experience. We cannot retreat into monastic or aesthetic individualism. What should we do about the areas of social relationships which we need in order to ensure communication between us? We need to be protected from all forms of dictatorship or of hegemony. The role of institutions is no longer to impose rules but to help us to construct the human subject out of the diversity of individuals and of social groups. Social institutions must permit and organize communication between the personal or collective actors, different as they are from each other, by providing an image of humanity which is not associated with any particular society. The social realm no longer belongs to society but has instead become that of relationships between individuals and communities, insofar as all of them seek to combine *universalism*, which enables us to live together with a respect for differences, without which the strongest would dominate over all the others.

Over the course of the last half century we have seen a decline in political passion, or in other words in our commitment as subjects to political conflicts and issues: class against class, nation against colonial domination or the feminist struggle against male power. With the decline of the industrial society, the key conflicts rapidly became those where the predominant issues were no longer focused on social problems but on cultural matters and debates. The current crisis, in this context, is more than just a crisis given that it accelerates the transformation from one type of society to another. But if entry to the new society is possible, the last social actors of the industrial society fail to understand the new social and cultural movements. Hence the striking image we are confronted with: we are going through a major crisis, one which may even have catastrophic consequences, yet the new political stage remains empty. The conservatives have been reduced to silence, but neither does anything seem capable of halting the decline of the social democracies, a situation which inevitably signals the disappearance of the political culture of the industrial era. As a matter of urgency, the social democratic left needs to transform itself into a 'post-social' left and the right must use state intervention to bring damaging speculation to an end.

Why this silence from the left, and even more significantly, from the intellectuals and all those once so involved in political debate? The explanation lies in the fact that, since no truly political debate can be conducted in isolation from social or cultural conflicts, the social democratic left, by proving itself incapable of representing the new subjects of the liberation movements, has deprived itself of any capacity for political action.

It is by setting this breakdown between the system and the subject in a historical context that we can best reach a conclusion, since a great many of the ideas used here are of a historical nature. What gave the industrial society a central place in sociological analysis is that it represented the moment when integration between economic and social categories was at its height. Class, as a social category, was inseparable from the class struggle, determined by an exploitative economic relationship. But it would be a mistake to believe that this situation is normal and that the others are merely the result of the crisis.

Before the industrial period, as I have emphasized, society analysed itself in *political* terms, and equally it was political power that favoured the expansion of the capitalist economy. It was also in political terms that the revolutionary movements which cast out kings in the name of the nation, of the republic and of the people, came into being. This version of social reality endured for a long time in countries where industrialization was slower in coming, as was the case in Russia where Lenin suppressed the mass Menshevik unionism in favour of the Bolshevik party and installed the soviet regime in power, by means of a coup d'état.

Amongst the industrial societies, certain countries, such as France, favoured giving a central role to political action, and it was Jules Guesde who in 1905 defeated Jean Jaurès in the leadership elections for the new socialist party. In an even more dramatic manner, at the congress of Tours in 1920, the Leninists claimed victory over the Socialists, who were less committed to state control.

Today too, many countries, at the risk of falling even further behind, seek to maintain class relationships dating back to the industrial society at the heart of their social fabric, just as they also refuse to see anything other than the political dimension of social conflicts. This is the case in many countries which were not directly involved in industrial revolutions.

What they failed to notice is the growing separation of economic and social categories, which I have highlighted in this book and in a number of previous works. This separation does not mean a return to pre-industrial societies and to their voluntarism, either by states or by entrepreneurs. On the contrary, with the support of new communication techniques, the economic system dominated by globalization is increasingly controlled by financial capitalism, which detaches itself from all the social and political aspects of economic life to focus exclusively on maximum profit. On the other hand, those actors who before becoming economic or social actors had previously been political ones can now only count on themselves and on their *rights* to lend legitimacy to their demands, since the social sphere is being rapidly destroyed by economic globalization.

The current crisis is witnessing the disappearance of the actors of the industrial society. The financiers cut themselves off from even the largest manufacturing companies. Those unions with communist leanings have been crushed by the stranglehold of the Soviet Union. As for other unions, their weakness is largely the result of the fragmentation which has affected the active population.

If the crisis is not the principal cause of these changes, it is because it represents a long-term trend which has broken the links between both financial and industrial capitalism with business leaders or workers, with their common culture and state interventions. The crisis does indeed represent a breakdown, and one which is not confined to the increased separation between the financial world and that of production, insofar as it shatters the industrial logic, or in other words, the interdependence – or even fusion – of economic and social categories.

Instead of halting the long-term transformation of society, the crisis has accelerated it, abruptly severing the links between the economy and society which had become more and more strained since the triumph of neoliberalism in the first half of the 1970s. Consequently, we cannot hope to recover from this crisis unless we understand that only an appeal to the universal rights of the human subject can halt the destruction of society by the globalized economy. At the end of June 2010, the hypothesis of a fall in the euro gained strength, although the means of avoiding such a scenario remain the same.

This immense task cannot be achieved through a revolution, for all revolutions crush social demands in favour of an implacable logic, inherent in the very nature of things, in the way capitalism functions or in the force of arms.

Even less can it be achieved through the kind of reforms proposed by the social democrats, who are already showing signs of exhaustion only a generation after the final collapse of the Soviet Union and of communism.

This task can only be carried through to a successful conclusion by militants and certain key figures who are organized not on a vertical model, like the parties and the unions, but horizontally by means of public opinion and by actors who are informed above all by the media and the internet and who are determined to prevent the emergence of any new power which will be more authoritarian than the old one.

These individuals and groups are motivated by their determination to be guided only by their own commitment to the defence of rights for all and of all, including those of the environment, which is under threat from current industrial and agricultural methods. Only a deep sense of conviction, reinforced by a passion for life and liberty, will be powerful enough to sweep away all the obstacles hampering the creation of a new society.

To shrink before such a task and to settle instead for restoring order in economic life can lead only to failure and to yet more crises.

# Summary

In the interests of clarity, I would like to briefly set out some principal conclusions:

– My *first conclusion* is that we are not dealing here with either a class struggle or a contest between social categories. The crisis is the result of the *breakdown* imposed by the financiers between their interests and those of the population as a whole. The capitalist industrial society, which contained within it the means to defend workers' interests, as well as a degree of protection for financiers and business leaders, was destroyed by the irresponsible actions of certain financiers. Our first goal must be the reconstruction of a society in which *the masters of the economy will be obliged by the state to respect the responses and interests of the population.*

Some believe we need to embark once again on the path of reforms and revive social democracy. I no longer agree: half-measures are no use today when the priority must be to ensure that the behaviour which triggered the crisis is no longer possible. Already the financiers, having recovered their strength, are trying to reconstruct a parallel financial system which is far less tightly controlled than the activities of stock exchanges. I do not choose to take a radical position; I simply accept it, because there is no alternative and because we are no better placed today than we were yesterday to resolve problems by means of negotiations. Our institutions are as incapable of solving economic problems as they are environmental ones.

– A *second conclusion*, which is easier to accept, is that any return to the past is impossible, since the crisis was provoked by behaviour which turned its back on rational control. Industrial societies were mortally wounded; *they cannot be brought back to life*.

– My *third conclusion* is that our *only choice* is: either to resign ourselves to repeated crises until some final catastrophe occurs, or else to reconstruct a *new type* of economic and social fabric. It is not a matter of choosing between the present and the past but between an ongoing series of crises and a project to construct new social relationships and new institutions.

– This is why my *fourth conclusion* is the most important. Faced with an increasingly globalized economic universe, the only possible line of defence must lie *beyond* the economic and social reality, on a level beyond the reach of any social or political force which is at least equal to that on which the global economic system has taken shape. This involves an appeal to *universal rights for every human being*: the right to life, the right to freedom and the recognition of this freedom by others, and also the right to enjoy social and cultural bonds which are threatened by the inhuman universe of profit. In every street and in every town we hear the same cry: 'I want to be *respected*'; 'I do not want to be *humiliated* any longer'. A moral argument against an economic one: the social fabric, weakened or torn apart by financial capitalism, in fact conflicts with the interests of the population as a whole. We need above all to revive a policy which respects the demands of all human beings. There is no direct clash between two opposing social forces, such as existed in the past, and especially in the early days of industrial societies. Yet we still continue to see the economic universe treat human beings as though they were products or machines.

This confrontation between two principles situated above and beyond society can lead to a 'war of gods' as Max Weber put it. In that case, everybody's lives would be dominated by violence and by all the consequences of the demise of the actors.

– My *fifth conclusion*, therefore, is that the broad idea of respect for human rights must be urgently transformed into new forms of social relationships which are dynamic and not just a matter of law. We must also re-invigorate women's movements and the case for sustainable development.

All these conclusions correspond to different elements of the analysis, but at the same time they form a whole which provides a clear definition of the consequences of crises and therefore of the means to avoid them.

Since an economic crisis is essentially the breakdown of an economic and social system, in other words of social relations geared to specific aims and kept going by public interventions, the most effective response to a crisis is *the reconstruction of relations between the economic actors, the establishment of a set of shared values, and new public interventions.*

What makes this reconstruction possible is that, for the most part, the actors are not motivated only by the pursuit of their own interests. This in no way diminishes the importance of anti-cyclical policies and of controls applied to financial activities. But it is high time to acknowledge that a crisis is much more than a mechanical breakdown and that it is the general state of the social fabric which contributes either to an exacerbation of the crisis, or to social and economic recovery. Above all, it must be emphasized that democracy, which transforms workers into responsible citizens, is the essential condition for economic and social recovery, at least in countries which have already chosen political freedom over totalitarianism.

We have gained freedoms and now we must defend them. But we must also create a movement which, based on the demands and claims of the majority, is capable of breathing new life into the political world even as it controls it.

# Bibliography

Aglietta, M., *La crise. Pourquoi en est-on arrivé là? Comment en sortir?* Paris, Michalon, 2008.

Aglietta, M. and Berrebi, L., *Désordres dans le capitalisme mondial*, Paris, Odile Jacob, 2007.

Aglietta, M. and Rigot, S., *Crise et rénovation de la finance*, Paris, Odile Jacob, 2009.

Albert, M., 1991, *Capitalisme contre capitalisme*, Paris, Seuil, series 'Points', 1998.

Alinsky, S., *Reveille for Radicals*, Chicago, University of Chicago Press, 1946; 2nd edn, New York, Vintage Books, 1969.

Arendt, H., 1951, *Les Origines du totalitarisme*, Paris, Le Seuil, 2006 (especially part 2, 'Impérialisme', chap. 9).

Arendt, H., 1963, *Essai sur la révolution*, Paris, Gallimard, 1967 (especially chap. 4).

Arendt, H., 1961, *La Crise de la culture*, Paris, Gallimard, series 'Folio', 1989.

Arendt, H., *L'Impérialisme*, Paris, Fayard, 1982.

Artus, P., 'Le pire est devant nous', special issue of *Acteurs de l'Économie, Rhône-Alps*, November 2009, pp. 40–7.

Artus, P. and Pastré O., *Sorties de crise: ce qu'on ne nous dit pas, et ce qui nous attend*, Paris, Perrin, 2009 (especially parts 2 and 4).

Attali, J., 2008, *La Crise, et après?* Paris, Fayard, new edition, 2009.

Baudrillard, J., *La Pacte de lucidité ou l'intelligence du Mal*, Paris, Galilée, 2004.

Bauman, Z., *Le Coût humain de la mondialisation*, Paris, Hachette, 1999.

Bauman, Z., *In Search of Politics*, Stanford, CA, Stanford University Press, 1999.

Bauman, Z., 2002, *La Société assiégée*, Rodez, Le Rouergue-Chambon, 2005 (especially part 1, pp. 41–167).

Bauman, Z., *Vies perdues: la modernité et ses exclus*, Paris, Payot, 2006.

Bavarez, N., *Après le déluge. La grande crise de la mondialisation*, Paris, Perrin, 2009.

Beck, U., *Pouvoir et Contre-Pouvoir à l'heure de la mondialisation*, Paris, Flammarion, series 'Champs', 2003 (especially chaps 6, 7 and 8).

Bell, D., *Vers la société post-industrielle: essai de prospective sociologique*, Paris, Robert Laffont, 1973.

Berlin, I., Mathieu, V., Sen, A., Vittamo, G. and Veca, S., *La dimensione etica nelle società contemporanee*, Turin, Fondation Giovanni Agnelli, 1990.

Birnbaum, N., *The Crisis of Industrial Society*, New York, Oxford University Press, 1969.

Bourdieu, P., *Combattre la technocratie sur son terrain, discours aux cheminots grévistes*, Paris, Gare de Lyon, 12 December 1995.

Boyer, R., *La Théorie de la régulation*, Paris, La Découverte, 1986. With many interviews, in particular with economists of the School of Regulation: M. Aglietta, R. Boyer, A. Lipietz and B. Billaudot.

Bresser-Peireira, L.C., 'The Global Financial Crisis and a new Capitalism?', *Journal of Post Keynesian Economics*, Summer 2010, vol. 32, no. 4, pp. 501–37.

Caldwell, E., *Tobacco Road*, New York, Charles Scribner's Sons, 1932. (French edition: *La Route au tabac*, Paris, Gallimard, series 'Folio', 1973.)

Caldwell, E., *God's Little Acre*, New York, Viking Press, 1933. (French edition: *Le Petit Arpent du bon Dieu*, Paris, Gallimard, series 'Folio', 1973.)

Caron, F., *Les Deux Révolutions industrielles du XXe siècle*, Paris, Albin Michel, series 'L'évolution de l'humanité', 1997 (especially part 3, pp. 333–467).

Castel, R., *Les Métamorphoses de la question sociale. Une chronique du salariat*, Paris, Fayard, 1995.

Castells, M., *Communication Power*, Oxford, Oxford University Press, 2009 (especially chaps 1 and 5).

CEPII, *L'Économie mondiale 2010*, Paris, La Découverte, 2009.

Char, R., 1946, *Feuillets d'Hypnos*, in *Fureur et Mystère*, Paris, Gallimard, 1983.

Cohen, D., *La Prospérité du vice. Une introduction (inquiète) à l'économie*, Paris, Albin Michel, 2009 (especially part 3, pp. 173–274).

Cohen, E., *Le Nouvel Âge du capitalisme: bulles, krachs et rebonds*, Paris, Fayard, 2005 (re the Vivendi, Enron, Parmalat scandals).

Cohen, E., *Penser la crise*, Paris, Fayard, 2010 (especially chap. 6).

Cousin, O., *Les Cadres à l'épreuve du travail*, Rennes, Presses universitaires de Rennes, 2008 (especially chaps 7 and 8).

Damasio, A., *The Feeling of What Happens: Body, Emotion and the Making of Consciousness*, London, Heinemann, 1999.

Dejours, C. and Bègue, F., *Suicide et Travail: que faire?* Paris, Presses universitaires de France, 2009.

Diodato, E., 'Dall'equilibrio di potenza all'equilibrio geopolitico?' *Rivista italiana di scienza politica*, Il Mulino, no. 3, 2009, pp. 441–64.

Dubet, F., *Le Déclin de l'institution*, Paris, Seuil, 2002 (especially part 2, pp. 305–402).

Dubet, F., *L'École des chances: qu'est-ce qu'une école juste?* Paris, Seuil, 2004 (especially pp. 53 and 89).

*Esprit, Dans la tourmente (1)*, November 2008.

*Esprit, Les Mauvais Calculs et les Déraisons de l'homme économique*, June 2009 (especially Dominique Méda, 'Quel progrès faut-il mesurer?', pp. 86–118).

*Esprit, Les Contrecoups de la crise*, November 2009 (especially part 1 'Après la bulle un nouveau cycle', pp. 13–55).

Fitoussi, J-P. and Laurent, E., *La Nouvelle Écologie politique*, Paris, Seuil, series 'La République des idées', 2008.

Fourastié, J., *Le Grand Espoir du XXe siècle. Progrès technique, progrès économique, progrès social*, Paris, Presses universitaires de France, 1949; re-edited, Paris, Gallimard, series 'Tel', 1989.

Friedmann, G., *Où va le travail humain?* Paris, Gallimard, 1950; new edn, 1963.

Fukuyama, F., *La fin de l'Histoire et le Dernier Homme*, Paris, Flammarion, series 'Champs', 1992.

Galbraith, J.K., *The New Industrial Estate*, Princeton, Princeton University Press, 1967. (French edition: *Le Nouvel État industriel*, Paris, Gallimard, series 'Tel', 1989.)

Galbraith, J.K., *The Great Crash 1929*, Boston, Houghton Mifflin, 1954.

García, N.E., *La crisis de la microeconomía*, Madrid, Marcial Pons, 2010.

Gore, A., *Earth in the Balance: Ecology and the Human Spirit*, Boston, Houghton Mifflin, 1992. (French edition: *Sauver la planète Terre: l'écologie et l'esprit humain*, Paris, Albin Michel, 1993.)

Habermas, J., *Une époque de transition: écrits politiques 1998–2003*, Paris, Fayard, 2005 (especially part 2, 'Transitions européennes', pp. 121–63).

Institute for Security Studies. European Union, *Managing a Post-Crises World*, Annual conference reports as working groups, 22–23 October 2009.

Jorion, P., *La Crise. Des subprimes au séisme financier planétaire*, Paris, Fayard, 2008.

Jorion, P., *L'Implosion. La finance contre l'économie: ce qu'annonce et révèle la 'crise des subprimes'*, Paris, Fayard, 2008.

Keynes, J.M., *The General Theory of Employment, Interest and Money*, London, Macmillan, 1936. (French edition: *Théorie générale de l'emploi, de l'intérêt et de la monnaie*, Paris, Payot, 1963.)

Kouchner, B. and Bettati, M., *Le Devoir d'ingérence*, Paris, Denoël, 1987.

Krugman, P., *Pourquoi les crises reviennent toujours?* Paris, Seuil, 2009.

Krugman, P., *The Return of Depression Economics and the Crisis of 2008*, New York, Norton, 2009.

Laacher, S., *Mythologie du sans-papiers*, Paris, Le

Cavalier Bleu, series 'Mytho', 2009 (especially pp. 47–76).

Lazarsfeld, P. (with Stanton, F.), *Radio and the Printed Page. An introduction to the Study of Radio and its Role in the Communication of Ideas*, New York, Duell, Sloan and Pearce, 1st edn, 1940.

Lévi-Strauss, C. and Charbonnier, G., *Entretiens avec Claude Lévi-Stauss*, Paris, Plon-Julliard, 1961.

Lyotard, J-F., *La Condition postmoderne*, Paris, Minuit, 1979.

Maldono, T., *Il futuro della modernità*, Milan, Feltrinelli, 1987.

Marx, K. and Engels, F., *L'Idéologie allemande (conception matérialiste et critique du monde)*, 1945, in *Oeuvres*, Paris, Gallimard, series 'Bibliothèque de la Pléiade', 1982 (especially 'Feuerbach', pp. 1049–85).

Méda, D., 1977, *Au-delà du PIB. Pour une autre mesure de la richesse*, Paris, Flammarion, series 'Champs actuel', 2008.

Morin, E., 1977, *La Nature de la nature*, in *La Méthode*, vol. I, Introduction générale, Paris, Seuil, series 'Points', 1981, pp. 27–48.

Moscovici, S., *Essai sur l'histoire humaine de la nature*, Paris, Flammarion, 1968 (especially pp. 5–46).

New School for Social Research, *Looking for Solutions to the Crises*, International conference, November 2008.

Obama, B., *The Audacity of Hope*, New York, Crown, 2006. (French edition: *L'Audace d'espérer: une nouvelle conception de la politique américaine*, Paris, Presses de la Cité, 2007.)

*Revue de OFCE, La Crise du capitalisme financier*, no. 110, 2009.

Orléan, A., *De l'euphorie à la panique: penser la crise financière*, Paris, Rue d'Ulm, 2009.

Pacquement, A. and Encrevé, P. (eds), *Soulages*, Paris, Éditions du Centre Pompidou, 2010.

Pastré, O. and Sylvestre, J-M., *Le Roman vrai de la crise financière*, Paris, Perrin, new edn, 2008.

Paugam, S., *La Disqualification sociale*, Paris, Presses universitaires de France, 1994.

Péguy, C., 1910, *Notre jeunesse* (preceded by *De la raison*), Paris, Gallimard, series 'Folio', 1993.

Pizzorno, A., *Il velo della diversita*, Milan, Feltrinelli, 2007 (especially chap. 5, 'Natura della disuguaglianza, potere, politico, potere privati, nella società in via de globalizzazi-one', pp. 309–40).

Polanyi, K., 1944, *La Grande Transformation. Aux origines politiques et économiques de notre temps*, Paris, Gallimard, 1983 (to re-read as often as possible).

Putnam, R.D., *Bowling Alone: The Collapse and Revival of American Community*, New York, Simon & Schuster, 2000.

Putnam, R.D. and Feldstein, L.M. with Cohen, D., *Better Together: Restoring the American Community*, New York, Simon & Schuster, 2003.

Reich, R., 1991, *L'Économie mondialisée*, Paris, Dunod, 1993.

Renaut, A., *L'Ère de l'individu. Contribution à une histoire de la subjectivité*, Paris, Gallimard, series 'Bibliothèque des idées', 1989.

Ritzer, G. (ed.), *The Blackwell Companion to Globalization*, Malden, MA, Blackwell Publishing, 2007.

Samuelson, P.A., *Foundations of Economic Analysis*, Cambridge, MA, Harvard University Press, 1947. (French edition: *Les Fondements de l'analyse économique*, Paris, Dunod and Gauthier-Villars, 1971.)

Sassen, S., *The Global City: New York, London, Tokyo*, Princeton, NJ, Princeton University Press, 1991.

Schumpeter, J., 1976 [1942], *Capitalism, Socialism and Democracy*, London, Routledge.

Sen, A., *Commodities and Capabilities*, New York, Oxford India Paperbacks, 1987.

Sen, A., *Éthique et Économie*, Paris, Presses universitaires de France, 2009.

Sen, A., *L'Idée de justice*, Paris, Flammarion, 2010.

Sennet, R., *The Fall of Public Man*, New York, Vintage Books, 1978.

Simone, R., 'Pourquoi l'Occident ne va pas à gauche?' *Le Débat*, Gallimard, no. 156, September–October 2009.

Smith, A., *The Theory of Moral Sentiments*, London, A. Millar 1759. (French edition: *La Théorie des sentiments moraux*, Paris, Presses universitaires de France, 2003.)

Smith, A., *An inquiry into the Nature and Causes of the Wealth of Nations*, London, W. Strahan and T. Cadell, 1776. (French edition: *Recherche sur la nature et les causes de la richesse des nations*, Paris, Economica, 2000.)

Soros, G., *Le Défi de l'argent*, Paris, Plon, 1996 (especially chaps 6, 7, 8 and 11).

Stiglitz, J., *Globalization and its Discontents*, New York, W.W. Norton, 2002. (French edition: *La Grande Désillusion*, Paris, Fayard, 2002.)

Stiglitz, J., *Roaring Nineties, A New History of the World's Most Prosperous Decade*, New York, 2003. (French edition: *Quand la capitalisme perd la tête*, Paris, Fayard, 2003.)

Stiglitz, J., *Making Globalization Work*, New York, W.W. Norton, 2006. (French edition: *Un autre monde: contre le fanatisme du marché*, Paris, Fayard, 2006.)

Stiglitz, J., Sen, A. and Fitoussi, J-P., *Rapport de la Commission sur la mesure des performances économiques et du progrès social*, Paris, La Documentation française, 2009.

Stiglitz, J., *Freefall: America, Free Markets, and the Shrinking of the World Economy*, New York, Norton, 2010. (Translated into French as *Le Triomphe de la cupidité*, translated by Chemla, P., Brignon, Les Liens qui Libèrent, 2010.)

Tarrius, A., *La Mondialisation par le bas. Les nouveaux nomades, l'économie souterraine*, Paris, Balland, series 'Voix et Regards', 2002 (especially chaps 2 and 4).

Taylor, F.W., 1911, *The Principles of Scientific Management*, Mineola, NY, Dover Publications, 2003.

Tocqueville, A. de, 1866, *L'Ancien Régime et la Révolution* (with *De la démocratie en Amérique*), Paris, Robert Laffont, series 'Bouquins', 1986, book 3, chapter 4.

Touraine, A., *Critique de la modernité*, Paris, Fayard, 1992.

Touraine, A., *Comment sortir du libéralisme?* Paris, Fayard, 1999.

Touraine, A., *Un nouveau paradigme*, Paris, Fayard, 2005.

Touraine, A., *Penser autrement*, Paris, Fayard, 2007.

Wallerstein, I., *L'Universalisme européen: de la colonisation au droit d'ingérence*, Paris, Demopolis, 2008.

Weber, M., 2nd extended edn, 1920, *L'Ethique protestante et l'esprit du capitalisme*, Paris, Flammarion, 2009 (especially part 2).

Wieviorka, M. (with Bataille, P., Clément, K., Cousin, O.,

Khosrokhavar, F., Labat, S., Macé, E., Rebughini, P. and Tietze, N.), *Violence en France*, Paris, Seuil, 1999.

Wieviorka, M., *La Violence*, Paris, Balland, 2004 (especially part 3, pp. 216–318).

Wieviorka, M., 'La Sociologie de la Crise. Quelle crise, et quelle sociologie?' *Cahiers internationaux de sociologie*, 2002, no. 127 (especially pp. 181–98).

Williamson, J., *What Should the World Bank Think about the Washington Consensus?* Washington, DC, Peterson Institute, 1999.

# Index